In the name of JESUS

PRAYERS FOR EVERY OCCASION

Omar Weber
Translated by Sarah Fields

Editorial
Concordia

English translation © 2010 Concordia Publishing House.
3558 S. Jefferson Ave., St. Louis, MO 63118-3968
1-800-325-3040 • www.cph.org

In the Name of Jesus: Prayers for Every Occasion translated from *En el
nombre de Jesús: Oraciones para toda ocasión* © 2005 Editorial Concordia.
Scripture quotations are from the ESV Bible® (The Holy Bible,
English Standard Version®), copyright ©2001 by Crossway Bibles, a
publishing ministry of Good News Publishers. Used by permission.
All rights reserved.

Cover art: *Hook's Head of Christ* © Concordia Publishing House
Manufactured in the United States of America

Library of Congress Cataloging-in-Publication Data

Weber, Omar R.
  [En el nombre de Jesús. English]
  In the name of Jesus : prayers for every occasion / Omar Weber ;
translated by Sarah R. Fields.
     p. cm.
  Includes index.
  ISBN 978-0-7586-2561-8
  1. Prayers. I. Title.

  BV245.W35513 2010
  242'.72--dc22   2010025012

1 2 3 4 5 6 7 8 9 10   19 18 17 16 15 14 13 12 11 10

Contents

Preface

Now Jesus was praying in a certain place, and when He finished, one of His disciples said to Him, "Lord, teach us to pray…" (Luke 11:1).

The disciples no doubt would have seen a very close relationship between their Master's ministry and His prayer life. Jesus' example was engraved on the hearts of His followers to such a degree that they could not even conceive of a life without the essential ingredient of prayer. Throughout the ages, the Christian Church has also regarded prayer in this way, leaning on prayer to plant new missions, to rescue those in anguish, and to praise God for His grace.

Perhaps we think that we have already learned how to pray, or perhaps we think that we still have a great deal to learn about the spiritual art of seeking, calling, and asking. This book does not attempt to make the prayer of the children of God something rigid and routine, but rather it seeks to be a guide that leads you deeper into permanent communion with the heavenly Father. It is our fervent desire that *In the Name of Jesus* will inspire you to come before the presence of God with the deepest parts of your soul.

—Rev. Héctor Hoppe, Editor

Prayers for Every Day

Morning Prayer

SUGGESTED READING: MARK 1:35

—◦◦◦—

Father of heaven, God of the daybreak, thank You for this new day. Thank You for caring for me during the night, so that I can awaken now to this new adventure in life.

Help me to live this day in fullness. Although things might not come out as I want, remain with me and guide my steps so that I know where to walk. Give me patience so that I do not despair, love so that I am not indifferent, and faith so that I will not give up after the first try.

You are like a good breakfast that gives us the energy we need in order to work. Breathe Your Spirit into me, so that I may begin this day with faith, hope, and good will. This is the pattern Jesus used so that each day was good. In the name of Jesus, author of the morning. Amen.

Afternoon Prayer

SUGGESTED READING: PSALM 141:1–2

———— ⌘ ————

Father of heaven, God of all my afternoons, half of this day is already gone. Although there are things that I have not yet completed, I know that You will help me reach the goals that I set for myself today. Thank You for seeing far beyond what we tend to take into account. Thank You for all that I have already been able to accomplish today. Encourage and energize me in this moment of the day to fulfill the responsibilities that still await me with the same enthusiasm that I had as the day began. Remind me that everything I do is for You.

Do not allow exhaustion to cause me to fulfill my responsibilities only halfway; instead, help me to be aware of my tiredness and to respect it as a fruit of the effort that I have put forth. May Your presence this afternoon make me shine with Your light, taking advantage of the warmth of the morning that is past. In the name of Christ, the God who makes all things right. Amen.

Prayer at the Close of Day
SUGGESTED READING: LUKE 24:28–32

Father of heaven, God of my nights, thanks for Your company today. Stay with me now that night is beginning so that my heart will be satisfied and content with the good day that has passed. Grant me Your forgiveness for the mistakes that I have made, so I may feel at peace. Remain with me so that the silence and darkness do not terrify me. Stay with me so that I sleep and awaken calm and secure.

The shadows of night invite us to rest, but there are those who must stay awake for their jobs. Accompany them in their activities so that they remain alert and productive. Keep vigil with those who stay awake, and send Your protection upon all those who keep watch over the night, so that we feel safe tonight. God of my nights, for You the light is the same as the darkness. Stay with us. In the name of Christ, our Master. Amen.

Prayer for Sunday

———⚬⚬⚬———

Creator of time, Lord of our days, thank You for this new week. Thank You for this Sunday, this first day. Today we may remember the beginning of Your creation and the beginning of our new life in Christ Jesus. Grant that the light that You have given us through Your Holy Spirit may brighten this day so that we fully dedicate it to You.

Thank You because the resurrection of Jesus on the first day of the week has brought us the possibility to start anew, casting aside our sins and calling a new week to life. Relieve us of the burdens that we carry with us from last week. Grant that today we may rest in the comfort of Your love, and that we may adore You and recognize Your goodness to us, thus dedicating ourselves to prayer and praise. Thank You for this Sunday, for this fresh start. Grant that we may be made new in Your presence today. In Jesus' name. Amen.

Prayer for Monday
SUGGESTED READING: GENESIS 1:6–8

L ord of our work, today we begin yet another Monday, a workday in which You call us to carry out our activities and fulfill our responsibilities. Make us look to the heavens that cover us so that we may remember You are watching us and are with us in all our duties. Settle the turbulence of our lives that we may breath easily, providing calm for the body and for the soul.

Give us, Lord, the good will to work and to remember that all that we do is for You and that we should do it willingly and with love. Give us wisdom to get a good start on our work, to be understanding with our co-workers, and to be enthusiastic about those things that are the hardest for us. God of peace, please help us enjoy this Monday as we dedicate ourselves to serve those who surround us. In the name of Jesus. Amen.

Prayer for Tuesday

SUGGESTED READING: GENESIS 1:9–13

———— ∞∞∞ ————

L ord of fruitfulness, thank You for this Tuesday. Beyond all our efforts, You are the one who grants the results and the fruits that we desire. Without You, all that we do would be in vain.

Lord, bless the work that we do this week through Your Spirit. Grant that our words might bring out the best in others, that our actions bring acts of love, and that good deeds flourish among people. Grant that just as the earth produces plants, trees, seeds, and fruit from its bounty, we would produce speech and actions that would help others. May what we sow yield the fruits of the Spirit and be a blessing unto the world. Bless, Lord, the efforts of this day so that they may serve the growth of Your Kingdom. In the name of Jesus, the God and Lord of life. Amen.

Prayer for Wednesday
SUGGESTED READING: GENESIS 1:14–19

———

L ord of light, thank You for this Wednesday. Grant
that during this day we may contemplate Your
presence and see the path that You want us to take.
You have a plan for our lives this week, and You are
revealing it to us. Let Your Spirit show us the path that
our steps should take. Guide us in the darkness of our
understanding, so that the light of Your Word may
inspire our thoughts.

Lord of this day, may our activities correspond to
Your will. May we work for our families and give our
best efforts, so that our words and actions may be in
accordance with Your teachings. Just as the sun brings
light to the day and the moon brightens the night, may
we be reassured that You guide and light the way so that
we may live according to Your will. In the name of Jesus
Christ, our Lord. Amen.

Prayer for Thursday

SUGGESTED READING: GENESIS 1:20–23

———∞∞∞———

God of abundance, on Thursday it feels like the week is coming to a close, full of all colors and shadows. Just as You have filled the skies and the seas with creatures so that they have life and color, movement and purpose Lord, fill this day with people and feelings that will make my life something special.

Guide my efforts and actions today so they may be meaningful, necessary, and useful for the growth of others. May my work and activities be in harmony with the creation that surrounds me, with my loved ones and friends. During my coming and going, help me to keep the commitments of this day without feeling burdened by routine; help me to enjoy them as part of Your creation. May this day be full of life and abundance, and may I seek Your presence and Your spirit in moments of exhaustion. Thank You for this Thursday, God of fullness. In Christ's name. Amen.

Prayer for Friday

SUGGESTED READING: GENESIS 1:24–31

———∞∞∞———

Father God, Lord of fulfillment, thank You for this Friday, the day in which You completed Your creation, crowning it with the presence of human beings. Thank You for the joy of the work that was carried out during this entire week, and for being able to place what I have been doing all week long in a good light. Help me to put forth my best, to complete all that I have set out to do this week. I know that with Your help I can accomplish it.

In this day, I can value the life You have given to me in all of its aspects: physical, emotional, and spiritual. I can do this because this is the day of man's creation and Christ's death, a death so that we have Your pardon and peace. May the joy of knowing that I am created and saved by You cause me to live a new life, guided by Your Holy Spirit.

Lord of this Friday, stay with me so that we can enjoy this day together. You have thought of me, and I also want to think of You. In the name of Jesus. Amen.

Prayer for Saturday

SUGGESTED READING: GENESIS 2:1–3

———∞∞∞———

L ord of our rest, thank You for this Saturday, a day of repose. This day invites us to celebrate the work of this week, to rest our bodies, minds, and spirits, relaxing and entertaining ourselves as we see fit. Thank You for the work that we have accomplished and the work we have yet to complete. Forgive me if I was negligent, so that I do not carry my guilt into the coming week. Cleanse my heart of the burden that it carries, so that this day may be a day of repose and celebration.

Thank You for this Saturday, a day blessed and sanctified so that we can remember how necessary it is to rest. May I think about You, creator of this Saturday, so that I dedicate myself to the enjoyment of all that has been created and produced with a thankful heart. In the name of Christ, who rested this day in the tomb, to rise with joy and power to a new life. Amen.

Prayer During a Difficult Week
SUGGESTED READING: MATTHEW 20:17–19

⸺◈◈◈⸺

When I look at the activities and meetings I have on my calendar this week, I start to feel anxious. I want to ease my schedule. I feel like my energy and my abilities will not be enough for what I have planned. Lord, how can I manage to get everything done that I have agreed to do?

Loving Father, Lord of peace and tranquility, give me unwavering courage to face the situations that I must undertake. May Your will for my life be my first priority in the upcoming days. May I trustingly bear my cross, as Christ carried the cross for me despite the pain that it caused Him. You will give me the strength, as You have always done, so that even though I feel overwhelmed, I will be able to fulfill my duties. When the week has passed, You will have shown me yet again that You are always with me and that nothing is impossible for those who walk with You. In the name of Christ, my Lord. Amen.

Prayer for a Long Holiday Weekend
SUGGESTED READING: LUKE 2:41–52

Lord, thank You for this long weekend that allows me to enjoy some extra rest. I am grateful that I can use this time for a trip, to catch up on chores at home, or to simply rest. No matter how I end up spending my time, I am grateful for this special weekend that You allow me to enjoy.

Help me to use the time well, remembering that my faith can grow as I spend time with others. Help me not to forget Your presence, whether I am visiting relatives, talking a walk, or meeting friends. May everything we do be to Your glory and for the good of our neighbors.

May Your peace be with me so that I do not plan more than I can manage and thus ruin this opportunity for relaxation that You have given me. Teach me to number my days aright, that I may gain a heart of wisdom, and may enjoy what I am doing. In the name of Christ. Amen.

Prayer on a Rainy Day

SUGGESTED READING: DEUTERONOMY 32:1–4

⌘

Lord of creation, sometimes You make Yourself known in Your power, and other times in tranquility. Today is a gray, rainy, and quiet day. My work has slowed, and my emotions are stilled. My projects are hard to finish, and I do not feel like doing anything. I am thinking about taking a break and allowing my life, like the dry earth, to receive the slow and gentle rain that falls from heaven.

Lord, thank You for this day. Calm my heart so that I do not live in a rush, like a summer shower that comes and goes in a flash. May I appreciate the different moments that You send my way and the transitions that each situation brings. Lord, open my heart today for what You have waiting for me to do. May I organize my schedule knowing that You are there in the details. Give me the ability to enjoy the days and the weather that You send. In the name of Christ. Amen.

Prayer on a Stormy Day
SUGGESTED READING: ACTS 27:12–26

––––⌘––––

L ord of rain and wind, be with me and protect me during this day of thunderstorms. Heavy winds, lightning, and thunder fill me with fear. Protect me from harm and danger during this great demonstration of nature's might and power. Protect my house and all the material blessings that You in Your great love have bestowed on me, as my life depends on You.

Ever-present Father, be with and protect those who are traveling. Protect those who live in insecure buildings and those who live alone. Every time we witness a storm we are reminded of our vulnerability in this world in the face of Your great power. But You are the Creator, and You can calm the wind and the rain. Give us peace to trust in Your presence and protection. You are with us, steering our boat, just as Jesus did. Calm us by increasing our faith. In the name of Jesus. Amen.

A Prayer at the Close of the Year

SUGGESTED READING: PSALM 90

⸺∞⸺

Dear heavenly Father, God of years past and years to come, thank You for this year that is coming to a close. Thank You for having been with us during the difficult times as well as on the good days. Thank You for the forgiveness that helped us move forward and not become discouraged. Thank You for Your protection and care, keeping us safe in the face of dangers. You have been our refuge during the past year, and blessed what our hands have accomplished so that our work might flourish and be of worth.

Lord, we pray at this year's end that Your merciful presence would go with us. Help us to be realistic when it comes time to evaluate what we have accomplished and what You have done in and through us, that we might not be discouraged by our failures or forget You in our achievements. Lord of blessings, You dwell outside of the realm of time. Help us to live wisely, following the teachings of Your Word, so that everything we do may be for our growth and for the salvation of others. Allow us to begin this new year well, with happiness. In the name of Christ, God of power and glory, who waits for us at the end of days. Amen.

Feelings

I Feel Alone

SUGGESTED READING: JOHN 16:32

———∞∞∞———

Dear Lord, I feel so alone today! I have sought the company of others, but everybody is busy with other commitments. I wonder if I have offended my friends or if I am so unpleasant that no one wants to be with me. This has happened to me before, but today, Lord, I feel especially lonely.

Maybe this is happening so that I will realize I can count on You. Even if my father and mother abandon me, You will remain with me. Many people have discovered that it is possible to be alone without feeling lonely.

Thank You for being with me, even though You are not here in flesh and blood like the friends that I have been seeking. Allow me to feel Your presence bringing me peace and joy. Let me make new friends, to think more about offering myself to these new people, as well as to the ones I already know. May I not close myself off from others or feel abandoned because of what is happening today. In the name of Christ Jesus. Amen.

I Am Sad

SUGGESTED READING: JOHN 11:33–35

Lord Jesus, help me with this intense pain of sadness that I feel in my heart. I know that even though You are in heaven, You understand my deepest feelings because You also felt sadness while on earth. Please allow Your Holy Spirit, the spirit of peace and of relief, to comfort me.

I pray amid tears and suffering. My heart is broken by what has happened. Listen to my cries. Aid me during my pain and sadness because I do not know how I can recover. I know it is not bad to cry—it is simply evidence of how much all this hurts me.

Heal my pain, Lord. May Your presence, O Lord, dry my tears and surround me with Your comfort. Thank You for being with me during this time. Thank You for understanding me. In the name of Christ Jesus. Amen.

I Feel Depressed

SUGGESTED READING: 1 KINGS 19:4–18

———⊶⊷———

Lord of the downtrodden, I do not have motivation to do anything. I feel all alone and without the energy to go on. I am tired, worn out, frustrated, and angry with myself and with everyone else. It is difficult to understand what is going on with me right now. Still, I believe that You are the only one who understands me, and I do not want all these thoughts to separate me from You.

Take charge of my life, Lord. Care for the enormous needs of my soul. Show me that I am not alone and that things are not as dark as I see them. Reassure me that faith still exists and that You are still taking care of me. Let me feel Your presence in some way, so that the strength of Your Spirit would renew my soul's enthusiasm for life. Give me rest and strength to renew my energy. In the name of Christ. Amen.

Everything Feels like a Routine to Me
SUGGESTED READING: ECCLESIASTES 1:3–10

———∞∞∞———

Lord of the days, I am bored with life's routine. Each day feels the same. I get up, go to work, eat lunch, come home, do chores, sleep, and the next day it is the same story. How boring! I feel so unhappy with this routine, but I am not motivated to change or to try something new. Why do I feel so dissatisfied? Why can I not take pleasure in what I do?

Help me, Lord, by curing this negative attitude that is enslaving me day by day. Allow me to see the purpose in what I am doing and to enjoy it. Allow me to change in the things that I can do differently, to take a vacation, to challenge myself with something new, and to enjoy the simple things in life. It is my outlook, Lord, and not the way things are. I want to see the value of life again, the value of the little everyday things, because all things are new when they are lived in Christ. In His name. Amen.

I Am Ashamed of My Past
SUGGESTED READING: PSALM 25

———◈◈◈———

Lord of restoration, for You there is no future or past that cannot be overcome. I humbly ask You to help me to get through this tough time. There are things that I have done in the past that I am very ashamed of now. I have hidden them as best I could, but they have gotten out anyway. Now, some people are using them to annoy and discredit me.

You know I have confessed these sins in Your presence. You have forgiven me because Christ paid my debt on the cross. I felt forgiven, but right now it feels like none of that does me any good.

Help me, Lord, to withstand this difficult time. I cannot deny what happened, but it is so hard to make others believe that I am not that person anymore. You have forgiven me, and I am a new creature. I still have weaknesses, but You help me to overcome them.

Loving Father, this is such a hard time. Encourage me and comfort me with Your Holy Spirit. I do not want to become hateful or desperate. Restore me by Your grace. May Your forgiveness be so strong that it would allow me to triumph over these accusations and this mockery. In the name of Christ. Amen.

I Feel Envious

———⚬⚬⚬———

L ord of all joy, thank You for everything You have given me. Still, there are times that I am not content with what I have, especially when I compare what I have with that of others. It sometimes makes me angry to see how people who do not respect Your Law prosper, even when they mock You!

Lord, I know these feelings are not good. They bring me pain and bitterness. You remind me in Your Word that everyone will receive his or her reward in the end, but I need Your help and stronger faith to free me from this anxiety. I need wisdom to understand that life is not just about having lots of things. Help me to see life in another way, with freedom and joy. May this jealousy disappear from my mind and heart, and may I learn to live happily in times of abundance and in times of need. In the name of Christ. Amen.

I Feel Discriminated Against

SUGGESTED READING: JAMES 2:1–13

—∞—

Lord of equality, thank You for treating us all the same, without playing favorites. Even though we are all sinners before You, and You offer us all forgiveness in Christ, we do not always treat equally.

Today I felt this discrimination to my core. I do not know why I was left out. Maybe it was because of my appearance, my words or my lack of training, but this feeling of being slighted has torn me apart. I felt like a leper whom everyone avoids looking at, talking to, or touching.

Perhaps I have done the same thing to others as they did to me today. Forgive me, Lord, for the sin of hurting others without realizing how much discrimination destroys us. Lord, heal these wounds that I feel in my heart. Jesus was also treated this way, and He overcame it. Give me Your strength of spirit so that I can withstand this pain and forgive. Lord, guide me so that this situation does not affect my social life and does not lead me to treat others in the same way. In the name of Christ Jesus. Amen.

The Comfort of the Holy Spirit
SUGGESTED READING: ROMANS 8:26–27

Lord of reassurance, there are moments in life when it is hard to find comfort. It seems like no one understands my pain and suffering. I am in one of those situations, and I need someone to help me. I cannot find the words to define and express the feelings I am having. But I believe, Lord, that You understand me more than I realize.

Thank You for being present with Your Holy Spirit. He helps me to understand the comfort that You offer me through Your Word and through prayer. He makes me believe that even though I cannot see or touch You in person, You are real and aware of everything that I experience.

Thank You, Lord, for Your forgiveness and peace that descend into my heart and relieve my sadness. Thank You for Your love and understanding that give me strength to keep going. Thank You for being with me in this inexplicable pain, when I feel like my faith is weak. In the name of Christ, my heavenly friend. Amen.

Fears

I Do Not Want to Die Yet

SUGGESTED READING: 2 KINGS 20:1–7

L ord of life and death, You have the right to take my life at any time because You are my Creator. But, Lord, I do not want to die yet. I know I am very sick. I feel strange pains and sensations in my body. The doctors do not say anything after they examine me. I never thought my day would come, but now I am begging for Your great mercy.

I cannot think of any valid reason to justify my request. I want You to heal me so I can keep serving You in the years that I have left. I feel great anxiety in my heart, and tears are flowing from my eyes. My time is in Your hands, and I trust only in Your great mercy because You have always given me what is best.

Hear my prayer and grant me this request! However, not my will but Yours be done. In Jesus' name. Amen.

I Am Afraid of Death

SUGGESTED READING: 2 CORINTHIANS 5:1–8

Lord of life, thank You for the promise of heaven and of a better life, shown to me through Your Word. Thank You for encouraging me through my pastor, for my brothers and sisters in the faith, for my family, and for all those who accompany me. But I feel afraid, Lord. I am so sick, and I am afraid to die. I have the hope of eternal life, of the wonder of meeting You, but this hope sometimes becomes faint because of my uncertainty, doubt, and fear. I want to be a good witness for those around me, and I try to be one, but I am afraid to die.

I know there is no other way to be with You than to be free of this mortal body. But it is one thing to say that and quite another to believe it. Lord, increase my faith because I feel so vulnerable. Help me to accept these fears and to talk about them. Hold me in Your hands, give me some proof that will calm me, so that my faith in Jesus Christ, who also faced death, may be stronger than any feeling. In His name I pray. Amen.

I Am Afraid of Failing

SUGGESTED READING: JOSHUA 1:7–9

L ord of all fears, I have been given a great opportunity for personal growth—a great challenge for the gifts and abilities that You have given me. However, I fear not being able to do a good enough job; it seems too big for me. I am afraid of making a mistake and of being criticized for not achieving what I set out to do.

But, Lord, I also know that You are beside me and that You will give me everything I need to face this challenge. I want to do Your will and to live within it. Lord, take away this fear of failure so that I can think optimistically and with faith. Lord, take away this fear of incompetence, so that I can think with hope and courage. Lord, remove my self-centered thinking and my forgetfulness that You give us what we need to meet all challenges that You set before us. With You at my side, I can face anything. In the name of Christ Jesus. Amen.

I Am Afraid of Going Crazy
SUGGESTED READING: DANIEL 4

᪐᪐᪐

Lord of sanity, I realize that I am acting like a crazy person. I am seeking my own glory and believing that everything is in my hands. I have forgotten about You and about all the grace that You have given me to be where I now am. That is why I suddenly feel afraid— afraid of going to extremes because of my pride. I fear falling from the highest place to the lowest.

Thankfully, You have caused me to stop and reflect on my life. Thank You for Your Spirit that is beating on the door of my heart so that I might see where I am.

Help me, Lord, to live with sanity, to give You thanks for what You have done in my life. Thank You, Lord, for the success, the honor, and the joys that I can see. I recognize that I have tried to keep them all to myself. Care for me, Lord, so that I do not fall into temptation. Free me from this fear, giving me the assurance that You remain at my side, so that I may act with humility and wisdom and not with pride and stubbornness. In the name of Christ Jesus. Amen.

I Feel Unsure of Your Protection
SUGGESTED READING: PSALM 61:1–4

Heavenly Father, rock of my salvation, thank You for the salvation given me through Jesus Christ. Thank You for renewing Your promises of protection and aid through Your Word and through other believers. Despite all that You do to strengthen my faith, I do not feel certain of Your protection. I feel fearful of what might happen to me. I feel like I am at the mercy of strange, hidden forces. I am afraid that my family might stop loving me; that my work and my business might come out badly; and that I may fall into sin.

I do not know, Lord, why I feel this way—as if at any moment something bad might happen.

Lord, I want to ask You to put my feet on a firm rock. Let me trust in Your promises, in Your salvation, and in Your presence that goes beyond the doubts and fears that I may have. Every time I seek You, I feel calm and I begin to trust again. Allow Your Spirit to make me aware of Your faithfulness that flows from Your love and Your grace. May I know that, no matter what happens, I can trust that You sustain me and cover me with Your wings until the storms pass. In Your name, Christ. Amen.

My Relationship with God

Fill Me with Your Spirit, Lord

SUGGESTED READING: EPHESIANS 3:14–21

━━━━∞∞∞━━━━

Lord of all new life, thank You for giving me Your Holy Spirit, who has made me believe in Jesus Christ as my Savior and has changed my life. He helps me to recognize Your presence in this world, and He gives me Your blessing and Your aid. I know that through Your Holy Spirit You make Yourself known and You work in the lives of believers, so I pray that Your Spirit would fill my life.

I want to understand the love of Christ in my life more deeply, so that He might motivate me to dedicate my life to Him more and more. I want to feel the power of the Spirit in order to be a more effective witness. I ask that You purify my life by showing me my sins, so that I may live in greater humility and holiness. Your greatness exceeds my understanding—I cannot control nor understand Your ways. I present myself with a willingness to be Yours. Work in this instrument that You have created, so that I may be more useful to You. In the name of Christ, who promised me His Spirit without measure. Amen.

I Have Asked You So Many Times!

SUGGESTED READING: 1 SAMUEL 1:9–18

———— ❦ ————

Lord, I really have very little desire to pray. You know how many times I have asked You for help with this problem, and I get the impression that You do not hear me. I think my life would change a lot if You would grant me what I ask.

I know that my promises and pledges are worthless in this matter. I do not even know if I will be able to keep them. So I beg for Your mercy and Your contemplation. Here I am in Your presence, stumbling over my own words once again. I do not even know how to ask. I do not know if my lips cooperate with my thoughts, but I need to be very honest with You. I have poured out all my feelings before You, and I do not care what others may think. I remain in Your hands, Lord. Hear my prayer and grant me the petitions of my heart. In the name of Jesus, I beg You. Amen.

Should I Keep Praying?
SUGGESTED READING: JAMES 1:3–5

———

Lord of my prayers, thank You for always listening to my prayers and petitions. I know that some of them are repetitive. Sometimes I do not know whether I should keep asking for the same thing because nothing has changed.

I know, Lord, that sometimes You test us to strengthen our faith, so that we might grow to have patience and fortitude, to make us more whole and perfect. But I do not know if I ought to resign myself to live with this problem for the rest of my life, or whether I should keep praying and trusting that someday You might grant me this petition. Lord, give me the wisdom to recognize the difference between what I can change and what I cannot. Help me to shift my focus from this one problem. Allow me to accept it as a weakness that I have to live with and to respond to it in a way that glorifies You. Help me with Your Holy Spirit. He is the source of my comfort and strength. In the name of Christ. Amen.

I Have Prayed So Many Times and You Do Not Respond

SUGGESTED READING: PSALM 13

———❧———

Lord of my prayers and pleas, I know that You hear my prayers. Your power and wisdom are limitless. But I do not know why You do not respond to me. It seems like when I have the greatest need and am suffering the most, You forget about me. I do not really feel like continuing this plea. Why have You not responded to me, Lord?

I have learned to respect Your timing, and I have learned to be patient and to accept that You have a purpose when You ask us to pray in faith. I ask Your forgiveness for my sins, as I may have offended You and that may be interfering with my prayers. Increase my faith, as perhaps that is the missing ingredient in my prayers. Lead me in Your will, if my request is not in keeping with Your purpose for my life. But please, Lord, give me a response. I am afraid of making a mistake. Help me to pray like Jesus, asking that Your will be done and not mine. I ask this in His name. Amen.

Teach Me to Pray

SUGGESTED READING: MATTHEW 6:5–15

———— ❧ ————

Lord of the heavens, I do not know how to pray well. It is hard for me to talk with You and express to You what I feel and want. It could be because no one taught me how, or perhaps I think that all prayers must follow a formula or model for You to hear them.

You want me to pray with sincerity and with faith. I want to pray like that, but I lack constancy; I am not convinced, and I need to know how real You are.

Lord, teach me how to pray. You do not have to teach me what to say, but simply show me how to enjoy the moments that I spend with You. Let me pour out what I feel without being afraid. May I praise You without shame, and may I be surprised in Your presence.

Beyond the silences, beyond my stumbling words and phrases that are sometimes not well put together, Lord, teach me to pray in that marvelous art of being with You and enjoying a pleasant conversation between friends. From my heart to Yours, and from Your heart to mine. In the name of Christ Jesus. Amen.

Before Reading the Bible

⸺⸙⸻

Lord of revelation, thank You for this time that You have given me to read Your Word. Open my mind and my understanding so that as I read it I may hear Your voice. May Your words reach into the depths of my soul and bring forth the best in me. If there are mistakes that I need to recognize, produce in me the repentance that I need. If there are truths that I should learn, convince me of them. If I need to be strengthened, motivate me.

May this encounter that I am going to have with You through Your Word cause me to praise You and to talk about You with those who surround me. Teach me to be a good person who is equipped to serve and to help my neighbors. Bless all those who read Your Word, so that in it they may find guidance for their lives according to Your will. In the name of Christ Jesus. Amen.

I Do Not Understand What the Bible Says

SUGGESTED READING: LUKE 24:44–49

—◆—

L ord of heaven, You reveal Yourself through the Holy Scriptures. Thank You for letting me hear and read the Bible at all times. Thank You for all the supplemental material that is published so that many might better understand Your teaching. But there are times, Lord, when I do not understand Your Word. I do not know if it is my clumsiness and lack of understanding, or my lack of training in this area. I do not always understand its meaning and significance.

You are able to open my understanding through Your Holy Spirit. Lord, I want to ask You to enlighten my mind. Take away everything that weakens my understanding. Allow me to humbly research and ask about everything I do not understand. Lord, You want us to know You through the revelation of Your Word. Bless me so it may be so. In the name of Christ, my guide and my teacher. Amen.

Prayer for Protection from Bad Influences
SUGGESTED READING: 1 JOHN 2:15–17

Heavenly Father, protector of our faith, thank You for the presence and help of Your Holy Spirit. Through the knowledge that You grant us through Your Word, You help to keep us from the devil's trickery and cunning. Protect us from the bad influences of this world that seem so tempting to our eyes. Keep us alert for traps that are hidden within certain people and things, and protect us from evil.

There are many things that surround and tempt us. There are many things that our eyes covet; arrogance and vanity surround us. The desires of our bodies are very strong, and we even believe that we will not be happy if we do not follow the ways of the world. Protect us, Lord. Motivate us to be disciplined in reading Your Word and in prayer, so that we may have the strength and wisdom we need to overcome the evils of the world. Your will endures forever. Let us remember and remain in that truth. In the name of Christ Jesus, the fullness of our life. Amen.

Suffering

I Am the Victim of Gossip and Lies

SUGGESTED READING: PSALM 31:9–18

—∞∞∞—

L ord of truth, I feel very upset because of what has happened to me. Someone has told lies about me and has tried to ruin my reputation. I cannot take it anymore. Even though I have tried to ignore the harmful things that were said, before You I can acknowledge that my heart is wounded and I am falling apart. How hurtful those evil comments and lies can be!

Lord, I beg for Your help. Give me Your comfort and guide me so that I will not isolate myself because of fear of people's lies and curious glances. You know me and You know whether I have done anything wrong. Forgive me my sins. Give me peace in my heart in the midst of all this turbulence. Make my steps sure, so that I can stand during these times of persecution. Free me from the enemy's attacks. In the name of Christ, who endured this and much more for my sake in order to restore me. Amen.

I Have Been Robbed

SUGGESTED READING: LUKE 10:30–37

Lord of peace and security, I need Your help because I am fearful. My belongings were stolen; even though they were just material things, I worked hard to acquire them. Protect me, Lord, from those who are willing to do harm to their neighbor. Heal me because I feel very vulnerable. Help me to forgive the thief and to release my own guilt.

I feel like I have been tossed aside. Others pass by as if they do not care about what happened, and I am in need of help from them. You teach us not to steal but rather to seek the benefit of others. Show me what I should learn from this unfortunate event. Do not let me become isolated and full of fear, but draw me to You in search of Your mercy and care. Help those who work to preserve our safety, so that they may find the thieves and retrieve what was taken. In the name of Christ, the Lord of all who heals everything. Amen.

I Suffer So Much for Doing Good
SUGGESTED READING: 1 PETER 3:13–18

———◦◦◦———

Lord of comfort and strength, this cross that I am carrying is very heavy. I always try to do what is right, and I have high standards for myself. But I have suffered a great deal. I have been treated unfairly. I have been mocked and insulted because of my goodness. This makes me feel horrible.

You call us blessed when we suffer for doing what is right. You teach us that it is better to do good than evil. I am convinced of that, but I never believed it would be so hard to withstand the reactions of others. You suffered and withstood injustice for the sake of others. I am not even close to that. But Your example encourages me because You triumphed and were exalted in heaven. Help me to maintain hope; let me nourish my faith with other believers who are also hopeful. Encourage me through Your Word and strengthen me with Your Sacraments. In Your name, Christ Jesus. Amen.

Thanksgiving

I Am Grateful to Know Jesus

SUGGESTED READING: ACTS 8:26–39

—⊗⊗—

Heavenly Father, giver of faith, thank You that in Your grace and mercy You allowed me to know Jesus as my Lord and Savior. This news changed my life! Thank You for those who showed me Your Word and explained it so that I would understand. Thank You, Lord, for those who brought me to You to be baptized. Thank You, Lord, for all those who prayed for me to recognize my sins and to believe in You.

Thank You, Lord, for this new life that You have given me! Thank You for the peace, joy, and hope that I feel inside. You reveal Jesus through the Word and through the Sacraments, and through them I can follow in Your grace and love. I cannot find the words to express how grateful I am for faith in Jesus. May this motivate me to share with others the effect of this beautiful miracle. In the name of Christ, my Savior. Amen.

Thank You for This Book
SUGGESTED READING: 2 TIMOTHY 4:13

———— ∞∞∞ ————

Thank You, Lord, for showing me the joy of reading. I am grateful that every time I open a book I
can understand the spirit of its author. Thank You that
each book is an encounter made possible through the
written word. Bless the ministry and vocation of all
those who write good books and who seek the growth
of others.

Thank You especially for the book I have just finished reading. How many things have stuck in my head
and in my heart! These are ideas that I will be able to
use someday, knowingly or unknowingly. I thank You
because this book has been my friend and companion,
and through it I have been able to meditate on, enjoy,
rest in, and even travel through the world of the imag-
ination. The good things that You allow to happen to
me come from You. Thank You, Lord. In the name of
Christ. Amen.

Thank You for Great Writers
SUGGESTED READING: JEREMIAH 36

———

Thank You, Lord, for books that tell the history of humanity and that remind us of Your work in the world. Thank You, Lord, especially for Your Book, the Bible, that You allowed to be written so that we could attain knowledge of salvation in Christ Jesus.

Thank You, Lord, for the writers who have worked to hone the gift that You have granted to them. By giving their time and effort they express their words on paper in order to preserve their messages and to communicate them to other people. Help us to value the opportunity we have to read and write, and help us to cultivate that knowledge, knowing that by studying we will gain wisdom.

Lord, bless good writers and their works, so that good literature will be disseminated throughout the world so that it may enable freedom of thought—help literature to grow and to benefit the arts and the sciences.

Lord, remove our fears of leaving written testimony of our actions, because they are useful for us as well as for our neighbors. In Your name, Christ Jesus. Amen.

I Have Finished My Studies

SUGGESTED READING: DANIEL 1:1–21

❦

Lord of wisdom, thank You for the opportunity that You have given me to complete my studies. Thank You for this time of learning that challenged the abilities of my body and mind. Thank You for being with me and keeping me safe. Thanks to You I have taken advantage of my time, energy, and abilities. You deserve my thanks for this achievement because without You I would not have achieved it.

There have been so many temptations and challenges. Thank You for the wisdom You granted me to overcome them. I was able to use my knowledge to face the reality that surrounded me in order to make good decisions. Help me to never forget about You, no matter how busy I may be. You want us to learn and study, and You are able to bless our efforts. Thank You for allowing me to succeed in my exams and tests. In the name of Christ. Amen.

Prayer for a Vacation

SUGGESTED READING: MARK 6:30–32

<hr>

Heavenly Father, God of rest and recreation, thank You for this vacation. Thank You for the opportunity that You have given me to set aside my daily routine in order to restore my strength, my mind, and my heart. Thank You for these days of rest that I am able to enjoy. Help me to unplug from my usual routine so that this can really be a time of rest and relaxation.

Accompany me with Your presence because my rest is complete when You soothe my soul and spirit. Forgive my sins. Unburden my soul from things that oppress and bother me. May my thoughts find rest in You, and may I see You in the wonders that I neglect to admire every day. Bless these special days, days of enjoyment and pleasure, so that they may be for my benefit. In the name of Christ Jesus, Lord of the best days. Amen.

Thank You for Your Word, Lord

SUGGESTED READING: PSALM 119:97–104

Lord of revelation, thank You for Your Word. Thank You for the people who wrote down Your teachings and Your Law. Thank You for those who have worked on their translation and printing so that we can have access.

But above all, Lord, thank You because in Your Word You reveal Your will, and You teach me how to live. Through it You have made me wise in the obedience of Your Word, and You have allowed me to help others to know Your holy will. Sometimes I do not remember these wonderful values that You have cultivated in me through Your Holy Spirit and the Word. But through them I have learned to understand life.

Thank You, Lord, for Your Word. May I always continue to enjoy reading it, hearing sermons and messages, and sharing Bible studies. May there always be others to share it with, those who publish it, and those who preach it for salvation and growth in faith. Motivate me to find ways to work well with others so that they can have the chance to hear it, read it, and learn from it. In the name of Christ. Amen.

Things Went Well for Me Today

SUGGESTED READING: MATTHEW 6:9–13 AND
ROMANS 8:28

———⦵———

L ord of blessing, I am full of joy today! I am wearing
a big smile that radiates from the joy in my heart.
I am glowing! I feel happy! And it is all thanks to You.

I have had a great day. Your protection and care went
with me in every moment, and nothing bad happened to
me. I was able to finish the work I had planned. Nothing
I needed was lacking. All of my tasks were blessed as if
a divine hand were accompanying me every step of the
way.

It is so wonderful to feel this way! It is great when
everything turns out well. I am so grateful to You, Lord.
Thank You for being so good to me. I feel blessed to
have You as my God. I praise You because I have been
able to witness Your great mercy and kindness once
again. Everything is radiant when You show Your love
in this way. May You be blessed, my Lord. In Your name,
Christ Jesus. Amen.

Thank You for All That I Have and Am

SUGGESTED READING: PSALM 126:1–3

———⟨∞⟩———

You have done great things for me, Lord. You have filled me with blessings and granted me privileges, special treatments from Your hand! It is not because of anything I have done, since I do not deserve such blessings. I am a sinner, and I need Your grace and forgiveness like we all do. But You have made me Your child and You have bestowed me with countless blessings.

You have made me into a better person. You have led me along the best paths. You have given me the greenest pastures and the calmest waters. You have surrounded me with the best people who have helped me to grow into who I am. Thank You, Lord, for these blessings! Thank You for the education that I have been given, for the family and friends who surround me, for the work that I enjoy, and for the faith that I have received. Not everyone has these wonderful opportunities You have given me. Everything I am and have I owe only to You. How could I not give thanks and praise You for such goodness and blessings? Accept my praise and thanks for Your love. May my joy and praise be a testimony of how good You are to all people. Blessed are You, my Lord and God. In the name of Christ Jesus. Amen.

The Battle Within

I Have Fallen, Lord

SUGGESTED READING: ROMANS 7:14–25

L ord of forgiveness, I have fallen again! I am
ashamed to confess the same weakness to You
once again. My heart is heavy just thinking about
how I have let You down, and tears stream down my
cheeks. I am so miserable! I have such little strength
in the face of evil! I knew that it was wrong, and yet I
did it—and did it knowingly, and now I come to You.
Can You forgive me, Lord?

You know the times that I have come seeking forgiveness and the times I promised not to do it again. You are
familiar with my weakness and my body that falls into
sin. Because of the mercy that You showed me in Jesus,
I return to You. Despite my shame, my pain, and my
powerlessness, I only find peace in You.

Help me to grow in the power of Your Holy Spirit
so that I do not fall again. I trust too much in myself and
I am often negligent of Your forgiveness. Christ suffered so much to pay for my sins. May His cross inspire
strength in the face of temptation. Thank You, Lord,
for Your mercy. Thank You for the relief that You've
brought me. In Christ's name. Amen.

I Feel Guilty

SUGGESTED READING: PSALM 103:8–14

⸺⸙⸺

Lord of forgiveness I am in great need of Your mercy and compassion. I have let You down again because I have not done what I should have done, and instead I did what my natural desires led me to do. I see the harm that I have done to You, that I have done to myself, and that I have done to others, too. Your Spirit has caused my conscience to feel pain and profound shame for my sin. I cannot tolerate this guilt that aches all the way to my bones.

Lord, I need Your forgiveness. I know that I do not deserve it, but I come to You trusting in what Jesus did for me when He died on the cross. He invited me with open arms to recognize my sin and to seek Your love and mercy. Forgive this sin of mine, Lord. Remove this horrible guilt from my mind, take this anxiety from my heart, and remove the restlessness in my spirit. Give me Your forgiveness so that I can be at peace with You and can rely on Your blessing. I beg it in the name of Jesus. Amen.

I Forgot about You, Lord
SUGGESTED READING: PSALM 42:1–11

———∞∞∞———

Heavenly Father, faithful and patient God, thank You for remaining near me even in those times that I totally forget about You. I have the tendency to put everything off until later, even though I set out to be mindful of Your Word, prayer, and the Church, I do not take these things as seriously and faithfully as I ought.

That is why I am here now, in this sorry state, miserable, thirsty, and fearful. I do not know why this happens to me time and again. I am unfaithful, Lord, and even though it is harmful to me, I cannot manage to overcome this weakness. Help me to feel a daily thirst for You, in order to enjoy Your presence and to have Your guidance in the smallest matters. It is hard for me to seek You, Lord, but I know that You get my attention so that this will not happen. Let me know, Lord, somehow, that You are here. I pray this in the name of Christ. Amen.

I Have Not Kept My Promise

SUGGESTED READING: ECCLESIASTES 5:1–7

∞

Lord of all promises, You always keep Your promises and thus You show the value of Your Word. But I sin, time after time. I make promises that I cannot keep. What a weakness to not know how to overcome! I do not know if the problem is that I am too quick to speak or that I lack the strength of will to keep my vows. I do it with every intention of keeping my word, but later I am sorry to find that I cannot.

What is going on with me, Lord? Why this weakness? Help me to control my words so that I do not say more than I ought to say. Help me, Lord, to keep my promises, even if it takes a lot of effort. I know that You are familiar with my weaknesses and that we all fail. I know I am weak and lazy. But that is no excuse. Guide me, Lord, so that I grow in the practice of doing Your will. In Jesus' name. Amen.

Give Me Patience, Lord

SUGGESTED READING: HEBREWS 10:32–39

———∞∞∞———

Lord of patience, I appreciate these opportunities in which You have helped me to endure the unbearable. When I thought I could not take it anymore, You supported me with Your Spirit, and I learned what it means to be patient and to overcome shame.

Now once again I am facing a difficult test, and I doubt I can withstand it. I think my patience has already run out. I have had enough, and I have not achieved anything. I know You have had great patience with me and my transgressions, and that you ask me to similar great patience with those who are my neighbor. But You are divine, and I am just a human being. So help me, Lord, if You think that I can do it. Give me the ability to feel the love that Christ had for me, so that I can also have it to love others.

I hope this desperate prayer reaches You quickly because I need You more now than ever. In Your name, Christ. Amen.

I Cannot Bring Myself to Tell the Truth
SUGGESTED READING: 1 PETER 2:21–25

Lord of the truth, You have taught me that the truth liberates us and that lies enslave us. That is why I try to tell the truth day by day and not hide it. But this time, telling the truth may bring me serious consequences, and not just to me but also to those around me. I am afraid to tell what has happened. I am afraid to lose my friends. I am afraid others will be placed in danger by revealing what was hidden.

Jesus was always sincere, despite the consequences—the insults, mocking, beating, and death itself that it brought upon Him. I do not feel that brave. I am afraid of suffering for telling the truth, and I feel tempted to be an accomplice in this situation by just keeping quiet. Lord, give me the courage to obey You and the strength to overcome the temptation to remain disconnected from this whole situation. Give me the peace of mind that I need so that I can tell the truth with humility, knowing that I am also a sinner and not perfect. Teach me to be sincere. I know that is best, despite everything. I beg You for Your strength in the name of Christ Jesus. Amen.

I Should Be More Humble

SUGGESTED READING: PHILIPPIANS 2:3–11

———∞———

Lord of humility, thank You. Despite Your greatness and majesty, You became small to offer us salvation. Thank You for the love and the humility that You have shown me in Christ. Thank You for teaching me how to recognize my weaknesses and limitations and to not compete to try to be the best.

Nonetheless, Lord, most of the time I find myself humbling others and trying to lift myself up. Perhaps it is because of a lack of self esteem or the product of some sin that I cannot manage to discern. This makes me ashamed.

Help me to understand the value of humility and truth. Help me to feel the joy of Your grace that nourishes my soul and does not need to fill me with lies and bragging. Forgive me this sin, and help me to amend my ways. I want to be like Jesus. Teach me how. Please be patient with me. In Christ's name. Amen.

I Should Not Talk So Much

———

Dear Lord, thank You for my ability to communicate with others through speaking. Thank You for such a wonderful tool that helps me to grow, but it also causes problems sometimes.

Lord, I recognize that sometimes my words flow faster than my thoughts, and that has gotten me in trouble more than once. Lord, I have offended those who heard me. I have said things that were unnecessary and useless, and that have caused problems for me, and now I need to apologize.

Lord, thank You for giving me a certain ease with words, but I have to learn to speak only meaningful and necessary things that build others up. Help me to remember Jesus' silence; He did not respond or react to everything that was said to Him. Teach me to listen and to respect others' time. Help me to overcome this weakness! In the name of Christ Jesus. Amen.

It Is Hard to Obey You, Lord

SUGGESTED READING: JONAH 3 AND 4

———— ∞ ————

L ord of obedience, thank You for making me Your child and for everything that I can do for You. Thank You for calling me to serve You with these gifts. But this time I do not like what You want me to do. I feel like I am in a huge dilemma. You are asking me to sacrifice my time and abilities for a task that I do not think is worthwhile. I do not agree with You, but I am afraid to disobey You.

I want to flee in order to ignore You, but I know that You will come looking for me. You always engineer things to get what You want—Your will and Your ways are unavoidable! Help me to understand and to accept what You want me to do. But do not ask me to do it with joy. I will only do it out of obedience. You know how hard this is for me. I know that Jesus went obediently to death, despite the cup that He had to drink. Help me then with Your Spirit to obey You. In the name of Jesus Christ. Amen.

I Do Not Know Myself, Lord

SUGGESTED READING: PSALM 139

Omniscient Lord, Your knowledge exceeds all our knowing. You know us much better than we know ourselves. From our mother's womb, You have accompanied us in every part of our story. That is why I come to You, Lord. I do not understand myself. I do not know myself. I react in strange ways, and I cannot explain why. I am afraid of myself. I do not know my whole story. Others have told me little about myself, and I do not feel comfortable living like this.

Heavenly Father, I am not asking You to reveal mysteries that are hidden forever or that You remind me of situations that might have influenced me a lot. I beg You, Lord, to allow me to know myself and to accept myself. Control me and tell me the truth. Lord, forgive my sin and rebellion and make Your Spirit, which searches the depths of our hearts, give me the peace that I need. Help me to know myself like You know me. In the name of Christ Jesus. Amen.

I Feel Tempted, Lord

SUGGESTED READING: 1 CORINTHIANS

10:12–13

———— ∞ ————

Lord of circumstances and Lord of spiritual strength, how hard it is for me to resist temptation! I know that I should not fall, but I am thinking too much. It has captivated me more than I had expected. My feelings and desires are so strong that my whole being is against me. I know that this battle is against very strong hidden forces, and I am afraid of falling even when I feel strong.

I do not want to take this situation lightly. I can conquer these temptations because You have given Your Holy Spirit to fight for me. Show me the way out so that this temptation may have no power over me. Do not let me fall. Deliver me from evil because You always hear my prayers and care for my life. Make me victorious in this fight, just as Christ also overcame temptation. In His name. Amen.

I Feel Invaded by Evil Thoughts
SUGGESTED READING: JAMES 1:12–18

———∞———

Lord of purity, You know me well. You know everything I think and all that I feel. You know my deepest desires and my weaknesses. So I come to seek Your help. You know that I am vulnerable to certain circumstances and dangers in life that cause me to stumble.

My mind is full of evil thoughts and feelings that are accompanied by strong desires to sin. I know, Lord, that this is not good, no matter how much pleasure it might bring me. Free me, Lord, from these things that are harming me, even though no one may suspect or know about them. They make me feel ashamed and dirty. Help me, Lord, by Your Holy Spirit, to flee from evil, to seek a pure life, and to renounce these sinful desires. In Christ, who conquered evil. Amen.

Help Me to Believe

SUGGESTED READING: MARK 9:14–24

⸺⊗⊗⊗⸺

Source of faith, thank You for putting faith in my heart. Thank You for making me believe through Your Holy Spirit. This faith inspires me to pray, to experience Your forgiveness, and to do good for the benefit of others. How important and necessary faith is!

However, I find that I am skeptical. Even though I pray and ask You for a miracle, I really doubt that You can help me. It is as if I have lost hope.

But I do not want to be like this. I do not to be so pessimistic. Help me to believe. Help me to overcome my incredulity. I have little faith, and no matter how hard I try, I know that no attitude of mine can improve my situation. What should I do, Lord? Perhaps it does not matter to You whether my faith is great or small, just as long as I have faith and I let You make it grow. Well, Lord, here I am. Do what You want. In Christ's name. Amen.

Using My Gifts Wisely

Teach Me to Use My Intelligence
SUGGESTED READING: PROVERBS 2:1–11

—∞∞∞—

The more I study, the more I realize that I need Your help to discern what it is I ought to learn. There are so many books and facts surrounding me! I want to apply the knowledge I receive to real life so that it is not just information.

Help me, Lord, to take advantage of this time in life that You have allowed me to study. Give me wisdom and knowledge to protect my life, to help me understand the mysteries of humanity, and to defend justice and fairness. May learning bring goodness to my life, and may I share with others the things that You have given me the opportunity to learn and understand.

You have given me intelligence. Help me to use it with enthusiasm and to develop it as a gift that must be used in order to work well and to yield good results. Thank You, Lord, for this gift with which You have made my life more beautiful! I ask this in the name of Jesus Christ. Amen.

Help Me to Make Music

SUGGESTED READING: PSALM 150

⸻

Lord of joy and praise, it pleases You when we give You glory through music and song for all You have done for us. Help me to improve my praise. You want us to be creative and to find different and better ways to express our adoration. I want to use improve the use of the gifts You have given me so that I can play this instrument.

Help me to take the time to practice. Give me the ability to learn music theory and new techniques that will improve my interpretations. Help me so that with discipline I may work and develop this gift. You have given it to me as evidence of the presence of the Holy Spirit in my life so that I may serve others in praising.

Help me, Lord, to be patient with my lessons so that I may obtain the help that I need to praise Your name and salvation. In the name of Christ, my friend. Amen.

What Is My Vocation?

SUGGESTED READING: 1 CORINTHIANS 3:5-15

———— ∞∞∞ ————

Lord of all gifts, thank You for the opportunity that You give me to choose my vocation. Help me to see myself in a realistic way, recognizing my virtues and also my weaknesses. Help me also to see the world that surrounds me, a world in which You allow me to serve others and to contribute to their well-being. But especially, Lord, allow me to know Your will. You have created me just as I am with a very special purpose. You have a plan for my life, and I want fulfill it. Guide me with Your Holy Spirit so that I might choose wisely and without rushing, aware of the importance that my vocation has for my own life as well as for others'. I want to build something and to contribute my little grain of sand for the improvement of this world, wherever I may be, in accordance with Your will. In the name of Christ. Amen.

What Is My Gift, Lord?

SUGGESTED READING: ROMANS 12:3–8

———❦———

Lord of all gift, all believers have received some gift as proof of Your Holy Spirit's presence in our life. You have given us all the opportunity to help in Your kingdom by serving others. I understand and I want to serve, but I do not know where or how.

Because of this I humbly come before Your presence to ask You to show me the gift that You have given me. I have read Your Word and I have studied about gifts. I have talked with my brothers and sisters in the faith, and they have certainly encouraged me. Help me to not think more highly of myself than I ought. It may be that I am thinking of a gift that is too important, or that I am not considering the needs of others. Lord, make of me what You want. I have received a talent that I should put to work so that is useful and not going to waste. I do not know what Your plans are for my life or for the mission that I am to fulfill in this world. I will continue to wait for Your direction. All work is important, and all gifts are, too. It doesn't matter what it may be, Lord. Help me to feel content doing it. In Christ's name. Amen.

Anxiety

What Should I Do with This Nervous Tic?

SUGGESTED READING: 2 CORINTHIANS 12:7–10

—∞∞∞—

What do I do with this nervous tic, Lord? Day after day I notice people's mocking stares, and even though I try to control it, I can't, Lord. Why do You not take this problem away from me?

Perhaps for You it is not important, and You may even allow it for a special reason. If this is the case, help me to accept that this is how I am. Despite this infirmity or weakness, You have a purpose for my life because You have created me like this.

Give me patience and tranquility. May this nervous tic not have more importance than You have given it, and may it even be for Your glory. I leave it in Your hands. Show me what to do. I already feel calmer. Thank You for caring about these little things that are so important to me. In the name of Christ. Amen.

I Can't Sleep

—⊸⊱⊰⊷—

It is the wee hours of the morning, Lord, and I do not want to turn on the light. I cannot sleep, and I do not know what else to think about or to try in order to make it happen. I have said my prayers as usual, but there is something bothering me that I cannot really figure out. Darkness and the clock have conspired against me to make this night a tough one for me.

But, Lord, I know that You can bring me peace in this time of restlessness and insomnia. I trust in Your protection to overcome the fears that assail me regarding myself and my family. I know that under the shelter of Your wings I can sleep in peace. You protect me from snares and terrors, from pestilence and disease. You have sent Your guardian angel to watch over all my ways. So give me the faith that I need to entrust my rest to You as well.

I sense that You are with me, and my thoughts become calm; darkness no longer frightens me, and the time that passes does not upset me. Thank You, Lord, for being there during my nights. In Your name, Christ. Amen.

I Had Strange Dreams

SUGGESTED READING: GENESIS 28:11–22

———— ⟡ ————

Lord of our dreams, You reveal Your will in various ways. Help me so that my dreams do not disturb me. Many images and voices passed through my mind and disturbed my thoughts. Strange sensations and feelings that I can't describe prevent me from forgetting what I experienced.

I was tired. Perhaps I ate something that did not agree with me, or I experienced some things that were hard for me to process. I do not know, Lord, what it was that caused these dreams. I just know that they were foolishness. I realize that inside me there are many mysterious things that transcend my understanding and are beyond my control.

You know me, Lord, and You know what I dreamed. Guide me to understand what I am to learn or to forget what might be preferable to forget. May I remain open to Your voice and to Your Word, that the Spirit may give a gift to discern the will of God for our lives and to test things that happen to us against Your holy will. Calm my mind and heart. In Your name, Christ Jesus. Amen.

I Do Not Know What to Do

SUGGESTED READING: JUDGES 6:36–40

⸺ ❧ ⸺

Lord of our decisions, it is so hard for me to know if I am right or wrong. You have placed a great challenge before me, and I am having doubts. Is this something I should do, or does it just seem that way? Am I playing tricks on myself? You have to recognize, Lord, that sometimes talking with You and understanding You is a bit complicated.

I do not want to flip a coin. This is an intense interior struggle. So I want to ask You to give me clear indications of what I should do. It might seem to You that I have little faith, that I am debating back and forth about something that is already obvious, but You know my weaknesses and my doubts.

I am not asking You for a portent from nature or a voice from heaven, but just that You remain with me so that I feel sure about what I am doing. Help me to get rid of these doubts, Lord of all power. In Christ's name. Amen.

ANXIETY

Prayer before Travelling
SUGGESTED READING: EXODUS 13:21–22

Omnipresent God, You are not tied by time and space. I am traveling, and many anxieties and fears flood my mind. Each trip is an adventure that brings opportunities and risks. Protect me with Your power while on this trip so that I may remain in Your care and safety wherever I go, day or night. Bless the drivers of the other vehicles so that they may be attentive to their responsibilities.

Protect my home, family, and those who wait for my return so that nothing bad happens while I am away. Guide me to a safe arrival, because You are our pilot and with You we travel securely. If I have any inconveniences, give me the patience to endure them and to solve them in the best way. In the name of Christ, the traveling teacher, who always journeyed with You. Amen.

I Am in Debt

SUGGESTED READING: MATTHEW 18:23–35

I feel bad, Lord. My debts have increased a lot and I do not know how to pay them off. I thought that I could manage my affairs well, but that is not what happened. I do not know what to do. As I seek ways to solve this problem, I get myself deeper into debt. I need a light to show me the way to freedom. These debts do not just put me in a risky situation—they also endanger those around me. I am nervous, upset, and in need of Your mercy.

You have always forgiven my debts and sins when I did not have any way to pay You. You did it in Your great mercy, and You have taught me to also be merciful with others.

I want to pay what I owe, but I will need others to be merciful with me. Give me the humility to seek a way to resolve this matter. I know that You have forgiven me for my bad management. Guide me with Your wisdom and strength so that I can face these bad times with responsibility. In the name of Christ. Amen.

I Live in an Apartment with Roommates

SUGGESTED READING: LUKE 19:1–10

———✁———

Dear Lord, this is a new and different experience for me. I have never lived away from home before. It is hard for me to get used to this apartment—the atmosphere, the furniture, and the people who live here whom I do not know well yet. It is hard for me to accept the schedules, rules, the bathroom habits, or the meals. I do not know how long I will be able to stand it here.

I know that I need to be in this place because I have no other option. Help me to get used to this new situation. I have Jesus' example, who showed me that it is possible to adapt and that any house can be blessed and sanctified if we let Him live with us. Lord, I want You to live with me and to be my friend and confidant. I think I also have my annoying habits that bother others.

Perhaps, Lord, You have a purpose for me or for the people who live here. I want to be faithful to You and to live in accordance with Your will. Help me to be a good witness. In Christ's name. Amen.

I Need Help Concentrating
SUGGESTED READING: 2 TIMOTHY 2:4–7

Heavenly Father, I do not know what is happening to me. I cannot concentrate on what I am doing. Time and again I find myself losing focus and daydreaming. When I get back to work, I note that time has passed and still I have accomplished nothing. Everything still has to be done or has been done poorly. I try to focus more and exert more effort, but I am not making progress.

You know me and You know what is bothering me. Perhaps I need rest or I am lacking motivation. I am afraid I will end up injuring myself because I am not paying attention to what I am doing. Help me, Lord, to face this problem with wisdom and to be patient and careful in what I do. Sometimes we are not quite ourselves; we do not know what is wrong, and we can only trust that You are guarding and guiding our lives. In Christ's name. Amen.

Intercession

Prayer for the Poor

SUGGESTED READING: JAMES 2:14–17

⎯⎯∞⎯⎯

L ord of the poor, we are all poor sinners before You and we need You to make us rich with Your grace and forgiveness. As we have received this wealth, help us consider others as beneficiaries of Your love. Teach us to be good stewards of what we have so that we always have enough to share with those in need. May we share our time with those who need a listening ear and advice. May we share our ability to teach with those who need our knowledge. May we share the food and clothing that You provide for us so freely so that we may help others.

Free us from the social prejudices that exist in our society so that we may consider each human being worthy of Your love and mercy. May we learn to give without holding back, like our Lord Jesus gave to everyone without showing favoritism. May the message of the Gospel be presented along with the help we offer. We ask this in Jesus Christ. Amen.

Prayer for Teachers

SUGGESTED READING: MATTHEW 7:24–29

⁂

Lord of wisdom, Teacher of all teachersm thank You for caring about our education and learning. Thank You for our parents, who were our first teachers. Thank You for the teachers that You provide so that we can learn what is necessary for this life. Thank You for those who patiently taught us our first lessons, who read us our first stories, and who taught us to pronounce the most difficult words.

Bless our teachers so that they may teach with authority like Jesus did. May their lives be in keeping with what they teach. May they edify the lives of their students on a firm and strong foundation that will help them to withstand the storms of life. Give them patience with those who need more attention. Give them creativity to find the best way to teach each student. Give them a sense of satisfaction for all the effort they put forth as they sow knowledge in their students. Keep them from becoming discouraged, knowing that they can count on Your help. Bless all teachers with Your wisdom. In the name of Jesus the Teacher. Amen.

Prayers for Those Who Are Detained or in Prison

SUGGESTED READING: HEBREWS 13:3

——⦿——

Lord of justice, I want to pray for those who are in prison because they are accused of a crime. Help them so that their hope and spirits do not fail in this very difficult time. Help the authorities who must investigate do so with the right attitude, so that justice reigns over personal interests and desires for revenge.

Lord, You want us to remember those who are imprisoned or abused. May our thoughts accompany them as if we were also there. Help us to avoid blaming or condemning them without really knowing what they have done. Instead, teach us to listen to them and to help them to clarify their ideas. You are the friend of those who suffer for the sake of righteousness. Let them remember that they are blessed in Your presence and that You hold them in Your protective hand. In Christ, who also suffered the humiliation of imprisonment and the pains of detention. Amen.

Prayer for the President of the Nation
SUGGESTED READING: 1 TIMOTHY 2:1–4

———

Lord of all authority, no authority exists in this world without Your permission, since You are above all dominion and authority in heaven and on earth. You've permitted us to have this government and this president, with all their virtues and faults. The president must answer to You for the job he has done. As citizens, it is our duty to respect him and pray for him so that we may live in peace and tranquility.

So, Lord, bless the president of our country. Give him the wisdom that he needs for making the best decisions for the well-being of all the people. Give him the capacity to hear the pleas and to meet the needs of the oppressed. Protect him from the evils that afflict those in power. Free him from the love of fame, power, or ill-gotten gain. May he always remember that You are the Lord of all. In Christ Jesus, who always submitted Himself to the authorities of His time, respecting them and teaching us to understand the kingdoms of this world. Amen.

Prayer for the Elderly Who Live Alone
SUGGESTED READING: 1 TIMOTHY 5:3–5

⸺◦∞◦⸺

God of the orphan, widow, and of all those who are alone and abandoned, we beg on behalf of those who are living alone that they may experience Your company and Your care. Through prayer and through Your Word, may they feel Your presence. May the loving affection of their friends, family members, and brothers and sisters in Christ help and supply them with the care that they need.

Lord, care for those who live alone. Protect them from the dangers that surround them because of their age. Help them to accept their abilities and to recognize their weaknesses so that they can live these years in the best way. May they find creative, healthy, and interesting ways to spend their free time. May their lives serve as an example so that others may praise Your great love. Give us patience with those elderly people who need more attention and lots of love. In the name of Christ Jesus, who does not caste aside those in need. Amen.

Prayer for a Deaf Person

SUGGESTED READING: MARK 7:31–37

———— ❧ ————

Lord of the challenged, we praise You for Your great love for the people who experience any type of disability. We know you are able to open ears that have always been closed and to enable a mouth that has always been silent; that Your power exceeds our understanding. Yet You have reason for allowing what You do to happen to every person. We pray for the life of this deaf person; we pray that You would continually strengthen them to bear this burden in faithfulness to You and in love for others.

Teach us to communicate Your love in ways that are not bound by our limitations. Also, bless those who work to find ways to communicate with those who lack the ability to speak or hear; bless those who lovingly serve them. Your Son, Jesus, also sought the way to connect with us despite our impediments. Make His example of service and love motivation for us as me minister to this person. Give us faith to believe that You can achieve the impossible. In the name of Jesus. Amen.

Prayer for a Blind Person

SUGGESTED READING: MARK 10:46–52

———∞∞∞———

Lord of light and color, thank You for the marvelous gift of sight. I pray for the blind who are not able to sense Your creation with their eyes. Help them to accept this condition and offer them Your protection so that they can make up for this deficit with the efficiency of their other senses. Have compassion for them, just as Jesus took compassion on the blind who sought His help.

Allow them to enjoy the light that Your Gospel brings so that their spirit is filled with light and color. Allow them to see Your glory and to enjoy Your freedom. Help those who work to improve the vision of others so that they might develop new technologies and treatments for curing blindness. Father God, motivate us by Your love to have mercy on those who suffer from blindness and help them in all possible ways. In the name of Christ Jesus, compassionate God. Amen.

Prayer for a Person with a Physical Disability

SUGGESTED READING: ACTS 3:1–9

———∞∞∞———

Lord of all our paths, who blesses the feet of those who bring the Good News, care for those who cannot move about on their own legs. Strengthen their will and encourage them so that they may find ways to get from place to place. Help them so that they may face the obstacles they encounter day by day with intelligence and a good attitude.

Allow the mercy and spirit of service of those who surround them to compensate for their disability. Protect them from the dangers that may be present. Give them extra strength in their other limbs and in their body so that they can move about with ease. May they find in their faith the strength they need to accept and overcome the disability that they face. May they remember that each day as You test us, You also give us the strength that we need to get through each trial. In Christ's name, whose wounded feet brought us peace. Amen.

Prayer for Schools and Education
SUGGESTED READING: PROVERBS 2:1–15

———

Lord of all learning, thank You for the schools that have been founded for our education. Thank You for the teachers who daily prepare themselves to teach the children and for the youth and adults who want to learn. Thank You for all the parents who care about their children's future and who procure training in the disciplines that are useful for life.

There is so much to learn! I pray for the education of our children so they might acquire the intelligence and wisdom they need in order to choose what is right. May they have the opportunity to learn the subjects that are necessary for their intellectual growth, as well as the values that they need to have to be good people. May they especially come to know the wonderful salvation that You offer them in Jesus Christ. May the Holy Spirit guide their lives so that they may seek everything that is healthy, true, and honorable. Lord, allow us to educate people with integrity who walk in Your ways. In the name of Jesus Christ, the great Teacher. Amen.

Prayer for Those Who Are Alone

SUGGESTED READING: PSALM 102:1–7

—∞∞∞—

God of companionship, we pray for those who are alone or who lack good company, for those who have no family, for those who are sick, and for those who—although they may be surrounded by thousands of people—do not have a close relationship with anyone. Allow Your presence to help them so that they will not be sad or introverted. It is neither nice to be alone nor is it good. We really need good company, especially in the difficult times.

May Your clear and bright presence, like rays of sunshine, bring them warmth and light in the darkest and most solitary moments. May they speak aloud with You, knowing that You are closer than they can imagine. Help them, Lord, to overcome their limitations so that they may approach other people and form good relationships. You are a great and wonderful God who created us to live in community. Provide good companionship to those who are alone. In Christ, our God, who suffered from loneliness and abandonment. Amen.

To Commend Someone Who Is Dying
SUGGESTED READING: 2 TIMOTHY 4:6–8

———

L
ord of life and of death, of this world and of the
world to come, You hold in Your hands the years
that we are to live on this earth. You know everything
that will happen to us, and You bring us together and
help us to say goodbye. The moment has come for us to
part with a loved one. Lord, receive our brother (sister)
who is leaving this world into Your home. Forgive all his
(her) sins and heal all his (her) diseases.

May the faithful companionship of Your Holy Spirit—
who groans within us, beyond our own understanding, and
fills us with peace— give him (her) strength within. May
Your angels accompany his (her) coming and going. May
Christ's death allow us to understand the necessity of death
and of facing this painful moment so that our loved one is
able to rise again to a new life with You.

Lord of all comfort, fill us with Your presence and Your
love. Increase our faith in this moment of separation so
that we are able to see what is invisible and to believe the
unbelievable. In Christ, our Lord, who conquered death
and gave us immortality and new life. Amen.

Prayer for Peace

SUGGESTED READING: ISAIAH 2:1–5

※

Lord of all peace, great are the challenges we face in order to live in peace with others. Conflicts emerge every day; they escalate, and enemies take sides. These conflicts bring so much pain and suffering to those involved. We cause ourselves harm when we cannot live in peace or encourage unity and reconciliation.

Help us, Lord, to recognize our errors and sins and our inability to make and keep peace. Teach us to be humble in our opinions. Only in You do we find peace, through submission to Your holy will. Only You make peace possible through Jesus Christ. He is the author of peace, the only one who can make it come true. Teach us to cultivate the message of the Gospel, to sow reconciliation where there is discord, and to learn the importance of love, patience, tolerance and self-control in making peace. Give us good diplomats and ambassadors who can cultivate good relationships between nations. May they know how to make decisions based on merciful and just foundations so that we may live in peace. Teach us every day to live in a peaceful and healthy way. In the name of Christ, the God of peace. Amen.

My Work

I Am Behind on My Work

SUGGESTED READING: JOHN 5:17–18; 9:4

———∞∞∞———

Lord, I have so many things to do and so little time! You give us the time that You believe is necessary for each one of us, Lord, so forgive my complaints and my lack of joy in my work. I recognize that I have not organized my time well, and I have also not known when to say no when I was too busy. I left out important things like rest and nutrition, and now I am suffering the consequences.

But, Lord, I want to finish this work. Other people are depending on my getting it done. They need me to make the effort. Lord, give me the strength, the concentration, and the enthusiasm to get it done without worrying about how much time I have left. Jesus, in His great mercy, often sacrificed His time to help people who needed Him. Give me the conviction that He had so that I can finish my work. I know that the mercy for others is a miracle that comes from You. In Christ's name. Amen.

I Want That Job

⸻

Lord of all great challenges, I call on Your name as I face this new job possibility. It seems difficult to me, and I am scared. I know You often give us opportunities to grow, so I do not want to make a mistake. So show me Your will so that I know what I should do. My resources and capabilities for this job are limited, but You are able to do amazing things with me. I will be waiting for Your response and seeking it daily in Your Word, in the advice of my brothers and sisters in the faith, and in every circumstance I face. Lead and guide me, Lord, because I do not know how to respond. I ask this in Jesus' name. Amen.

I Have Too Much to Do

—◦◦◦—

Lord of all time, I worry so much when I do not have enough time to accomplish what I want to do. I know that You care for Your children, but my faith is so weak in trusting that You are in charge of my today and my tomorrow. I despair because I think my world will come crashing down if I do not do everything today.

Every day has enough problems of its own that there is no need to think about tomorrow's. Lord, give me the wisdom to live this day as I should. Give me the wisdom to delegate what I should not do, to set aside the things that are not urgent or necessary for today, and to discern what is urgent and what is important.

Teach me to concern myself first with Your kingdom with the conviction that You will take care of the other needs that occupy my mind and my time. Teach me to live like Your Son. In the name of Christ. Amen.

I Need to Delegate Responsibility

SUGGESTED READING: EXODUS 18:13–27

⁕

Lord, I have too much work because it is hard for me to delegate it to others. I am not trusting enough. I think others will not do the work as I would have done it or liked it to be done. It is hard for me to trust, but I have realized that I just cannot give any more. All of my work is in jeopardy because I cannot manage it all.

Teach me to delegate and to walk alongside others, just as Jesus did with His disciples. Teach me to learn that mutual well-being is something that we should seek to share, and I am not the "one and only" or as indispensible as I sometimes believe myself to be. Then I will be able to rest and to do the work more efficiently.

Teach me to trust You, to pray for others, and to make disciples who can contribute to accomplishing this work that is so important for us all. Thank You, Lord, and forgive me for having failed You again in thinking of myself as more important than what I am doing. In the name of Christ Jesus. Amen.

I Am Not Motivated

———

Once again, night comes and I realize I have not accomplished what I should have. I cannot blame anything or anyone. I am the one, Lord, who did not feel like doing anything. I waste time entertaining myself and I start to feel very tired; I tell myself that I will have time tomorrow or the day after. I have the perfect excuses to justify my laziness.

What should I do, Lord? How can I overcome this weakness? There are days when I wake up with more enthusiasm and motivation. It feels like I need someone or something to push me to get started or to monitor me so that I finish my work. I haven't had bad experiences with work. I just feel lazy, but I am risking my own job.

Lord, make me more diligent; may Your Holy Spirit empower me to take the first steps because I am fearful and ashamed of being found out, despite my good excuses. Help me, Lord, to overcome my fears. In the name of Christ Jesus. Amen.

I Am Starting a New Job Today
SUGGESTED READING: EPHESIANS 6:5–9

—⊗⊗⊗—

Thank You, Lord, for the opportunity to begin working here. Today is a very special day for me, and I do not want to ruin it. I am anxious to see how it will be, who my colleagues will be, and what the work will entail. But I am more anxious that I will disappoint those who hired me and expect good service from me. Help to calm me and to remind me that I am an ordinary person who makes mistakes. May I not become desperate if I make a stupid mistake.

Allow me to face this job knowing that I do it for You and not just for my supervisors. May I act with respect, integrity, and humility. May I work willingly, since everything I do is for You. I know that You reward good service and good behavior.

Lord, bless this work and this long-awaited day for me. In the name of Jesus Christ. Amen.

I Do Not Want to Work with This Person Anymore

SUGGESTED READING: ACTS 15:36–41

Heavenly Father, You created each of us with a unique personality. You have also given us different gifts and different approaches to work. You placed us together in this time and place to share a common task. I have always tried to live and to work in peace with others. I have respected their time and their routines. But I do not want to work with this person whom I no longer trust, whose way of operating—although perhaps useful in some circumstances—causes issues and has made things difficult for me.

I want to ask for Your forgiveness, Lord, if I have offended this person or if I offend You by making the wrong decision. I ask You to help me to respect this person and to not gossip or criticize. I think it is best for both of us if we do not work together anymore so that we will not bother each other, and that way each of us can follow the path that You have laid out for us. In Your name, Christ Jesus. Amen.

I Need to Learn to Work on a Team

SUGGESTED READING: 1 CORINTHIANS 12:21–26

Heavenly Father, I thank You for giving me a great group of brothers and sisters to whom You have bound me with the very love of Christ. There are a bunch of us and we have varied gifts. But sometimes it is hard for me to learn to trust in my brothers and sisters and to permit them to do certain activities. It is hard for me to respect their time and their abilities, and I tend to get overly involved in their work.

Perhaps this is due to my upbringing. I realize that my attitude is putting the work of the entire team in jeopardy. They feel useless and I am overburdened with work. You do not want division; You prefer teamwork. Lord, teach me to love and to respect my brothers and sisters. Allow me to see them as fellow players on a team, to respect Your plans, because You are the director of the work and You know how each one can best serve. May I learn to be quiet and patient and to trust others and forgive mistakes. Teach me, Lord, to work with others, for my own benefit, for that of my brothers and sisters, and especially for the sake of the work that You have entrusted to us. In the name of Jesus Christ. Amen.

I Do Not Know How to Ask for Help
SUGGESTED READING: 2 KINGS 4:1–7

Lord of those who need help, I need so much from You right now and I am not able to ask for it. I am ashamed because I feel like a beggar, like someone who does not know how to face life. Perhaps that is the case with me. Perhaps I have made a mistake and I am afraid that someone will reprimand me. But I do not see any other solution in this critical moment than asking for help.

Help me, Lord, to swallow my pride and to learn to ask; I ask You to forgive me as well as to help me. May I not be prejudiced or think badly of those who say no, either because they cannot or do not want to help me. They are not obliged to rescue me. I think that You want to teach me what it is like to be at the mercy of other people, or perhaps You want to show me the kindness of strangers. I do not know what Your intention is, Lord, but although the lesson is a painful one, I know that You will give me the strength to ask, seek, and knock on the door. Thank You for being with me and for not abandoning me. In the name of Christ. Amen.

I Should Quit a Job

SUGGESTED READING: DEUTERONOMY 31:1–8

———∞∞∞———

Lord of all strength, thank You for this time that I have been able to serve You in this job. Thank You for the strength, the ability, and the gifts that You gave me to carry it out. Thank You for the support in the difficult times and for the forgiveness and humility that allowed me to recognize when I was wrong. I am grateful for Your great comfort and strength and for the beautiful adventure that we have lived together.

But I cannot do it anymore; I cannot go on. My strength is not what it once was, and it is time to let others serve You in the work that is yet to come. I understand that it is Your will that I leave, and You are the one who is most familiar with all our days and how much we are able to give.

Perhaps I will miss these days, this work, and the benefits it brings me. However, it is good for me to recognize my limits and, out of love for those I serve, to step to the side so that others can take my place. Thank You, Lord, for giving me the possibility of serving You. In the name of Christ Jesus. Amen.

I Have a Job Offer
SUGGESTED READING: PSALM 127:1–2

———— ≈∞≈ ————

Lord of our work, thank You for this job offer that I have received. The challenge that it brings is interesting in many ways. It offers me the opportunity to work in an area that I want; it also offers me a better salary, a better schedule, and many other things that I need to consider.

But I know that no matter how much effort I put forth, if You do not bless what I do, I will not obtain the results I am hoping for. Perhaps this offer seems great, but it might not be from You.

Lord, for this reason I ask You to guide my deliberation. Show me with the wisdom of Your Word and the Holy Spirit what is best. May I consider the pros and cons of this offer with patience and careful thought. May I consider this without being afraid of failure because my whole life is in Your hands. I also do not want the financial perks to be the only determining factors in my decision, since they may fluctuate over time. Guide me, Lord, that I may choose what You have prepared for me. May the peace of knowing You are beside me comfort me. In the name of Christ, my best counselor. Amen.

Myself

I Should Take Care of My Body
SUGGESTED READING: EPHESIANS 5:29

———— ∞ ————

I t is hard to understand how the body works! I love my body and I give it everything it needs. But after eating and drinking whatever I wanted and not getting exercise, I am realizing that my body does not really know what it needs.

Lord, I want to ask You for wisdom, self control, and discipline in order for my body to be a temple of the Holy Spirit. I do not want to get sick or unhealthy. I want to learn to differentiate between needs and wants, so I do not give in to excess.

You have given us an example in Christ and the Church. He loves the Church and does what is best for her, and that is how You hope that I will love my body: feed it and care for it. It is the work of Your hands and Your presence that dwells within us. Help me, Lord, not to destroy this body. Teach me to care for it and to be responsible for it. May how I take care of myself be a testimony to the love I have for the life that You have granted me in Jesus Christ. Amen.

Are These Sexual Desires of Mine Good?
SUGGESTED READING: 1 CORINTHIANS 6:12–20

———❧———

Lord of pleasure, You have made me. You have given me this body that amazes me every day with some new sensation that I have never felt before. How many latent forces are dwelling in me that suddenly awaken with some touch, thought, or gesture! I do not know if these sensations that I experience are good. Sometimes I feel guilty for feeling what I feel.

These are very intimate matters. Only You and I know of them. What harm can they do? In all this confusion, Father, Creator of my body and Redeemer of my life, guide me with Your Holy Spirit so that I may honor You with my body.

I want to respect You and respect myself; I want to feel at peace and not have to hide; I want to enjoy these sensations completely in the way that You have planned for me. Forgive my sins and guide me so that I may live in purity, and give me strength to overcome temptation. I know that You want the best for my sex life. In the name of Jesus Christ. Amen.

I Am Very Tired

SUGGESTED READING: MATTHEW 11:28-30

I am very tired, Lord. I wanted to find a moment of quiet and rest to relax because I need some space to renew my mind and heart. I have been running around all day. I have worked without stopping. My feet, my hands, and my mind do not have more left to give.

That is why I am here with You; I can only find true rest in You. In You I can relax without feeling guilty for slowing my pace. Guide my thoughts and emotions so that they may find rest in Your grace and love. May this moment of prayer bring me calm, just as in Your embrace I find the forgiveness and understanding I need for my shortcomings and the strength and courage to continue my activities.

Your yoke is easy and light. Teach me to live that way! Lead me to green pastures and to quiet waters, so that they may give me the rest and the new energy that I need. In the name of Jesus. Amen.

I Feel Old and Tired
SUGGESTED READING: PSALM 71

———∞∞∞———

Lord of everlasting mercy, You have always been good to me. You protected me and I have reached old age. Thank You for Your great mercy. Not everyone enjoys this blessing that You have given me. Even though there are many things that I cannot do anymore, I can still praise You and tell my friends and family about the wonders You have done for us.

I realize that many people make me feel old and useless. Give me patience, Lord, so that I do not become bitter. I can see that my strength and abilities are not what they once were. Help me to accept these losses and help me to work on internal matters and not to worry about external ones. Allow that my behavior and my words may praise Your greatness and plant seeds of faith in future generations. Thank You for this privilege, Lord of all generations. In Your name. Amen.

I Have Lost My Voice
SUGGESTED READING: LUKE 1:5–22

———— ∞ ————

Why is it that, when I need my voice the most, I cannot count on it? Why are You isolating me with this inability to speak, Lord? I know that my body is an intricate machine that responds to so many different stimuli that it is difficult to understand it. Is it because of something I said? Is it because of something I should not say? Why have You left me voiceless right now?

Despite my anger, my lack of understanding, and how desperate and frustrated I feel, I know that only in You I will find the rest for my soul, which is choking on thousands of words I cannot express right now. I will make dozens of attempts to heal myself, but You want me to be at peace. Many things will not come out the way I want them to, but You are in charge of all that.

Give me the forgiveness that soothes my spirit, the patience to accept that I am not the lord of my life, and the faith to believe that You can heal me. I accept what has happened. What will You do by tomorrow, Lord? My only hope is in Christ, the Lord of the Word. In His name. Amen.

I Feel Sick

SUGGESTED READING: MATTHEW 4:23–24

———— ∞ ————

Lord of all health, I need Your help a great deal today. I know that You heal all the ills of soul and body, and that on Your own body You took on our sins and illnesses so that we might have health. I feel uncomfortable, sick, and weak. The doctor has given me a prescription to alleviate my irritation and the discomfort.

It is so miserable to be sick! I cannot do my work. My body does not respond like I want it to. I do not want to think about what caused my illness, but it is hard for me to deny my responsibility for my current suffering. Forgive me, Lord, for all the wrong I have done.

Help me to heal, Lord. Give me patience and self control through Your Holy Spirit so that I can accept this illness and follow the doctor's advice. Just as You have always been the healer of the ills of my soul, be my healer in this illness as well. Cleanse me and cure me from this condition. Be compassionate with me just as You have always been with all those who have ever needed You. In the name of Christ Jesus. Amen.

I Am Going to Donate Blood
SUGGESTED READING: JOHN 15:12–17

———◦∞◦———

Heavenly Father, Creator and Protector of life, thank You for inspiring the intelligence of those who have developed science and medicine to benefit our health. Thank You for making blood transfusions possible. I am grateful that I can help someone in need by sharing my blood.

You have taught us to love one another and to help each other in difficult moments, just as Christ did when He gave His life for me. Help me to feel the love and care that Jesus felt for me. May the love that motivates me to help someone in need transcend my doubts and fears.

Help me to be brave, keep me calm, and take away my doubts as I talk with a doctor or nurse;weigh on my mind and spirit. Comfort me so that I may be at peace with You, and so that I might move forward confiendtly and with good consciencewith the guidance of the Holy Spirit. Amen.

I Am Going to the Psychologist
SUGGESTED READING: JOHN 21:15–19

ord of our emotions, thank You for the human
body, this marvelous machine! It is a machine that
thinks, feels, walks, and believes. It is a machine that
sometimes breaks down, that needs maintenance, and
that wears out. You are Great Physician that cures all
of our ills, and that is why now I come before Your
presence in search of direction and support.

My feelings and thoughts are mixed up and confused,
and I have decided to see a psychologist. I do not know,
Lord, how I have come to feel this way, but I know that
it is necessary for me to see a specialist who can direct
me in resolving these problems. Lord, give my doctor
the wisdom that is needed to care for me. Help me to
trust the doctor's care so I can sincerely communicate
with him about everything that worries me. Take away
my preconceived notions and guide us so that together
we can find a way to solve this problem. In the name of
Christ, who healed emotions and guilt with His great
love. Amen.

I Have an Appointment with the Dentist

SUGGESTED READING: SONG OF SOLOMON 4:1–2

—◦◦◦—

Heavenly Father, thank You for having designed our bodies in such a wonderful way. Thank You for teaching us to care for them and to enjoy them fully, in a healthy way, like a person who cleans a house in order to enjoy living in it. This body is Your temple, and I want to care for it in the proper way.

Today I must go to the dentist to get my teeth fixed. I know that they are part of Your design. I know they have an important role in my nourishment, as well as in my ability to speak and in the beauty of my face. I have not taken good care of them for a multitude of reasons, and now I must assume the bodily and financial costs of that carelessness.

Give me patience and strength to withstand this treatment. Take away my fears and worries regarding it. Help me to withstand the pain and to trust in Your protection. Help me to be more disciplined in the care of my body. I know that sometimes it is uncomfortable and painful, but I trust that You will help me to get through the treatment. Thank You for listening to me and for always being with me in these small but very important matters. In Christ's name. Amen.

Before an Operation

———❧———

Lord of health, I am having surgery today and I am overwhelmed by many feelings. I want to be calm, despite the risks that I am facing. I ask You to reassure me and to give me Your peace.

Be with the doctors and specialists who will carry out this operation so that they execute it with the wisdom and skill that You have given them. Be with my body as I am unconscious so I am in a good condition during the operation. Comfort my family and friends; may they have faith that everything will come out well.

Lord of life, sometimes it is hard to submit to another's will, but I know I need this. I have learned from Christ that accepting Your will is always best, so I humbly submit myself to Your divine providence, knowing that You always do what is best in my life. Forgive my sins and allow me to feel Your peace. In the name of Jesus Christ. Amen.

My Favorite Team Is Playing Today

SUGGESTED READING: 1 CORINTHIANS 10:31–33

———⚬⚬⚬———

Lord of all joy, I do not know if I should pray to You about this matter. I know that You hear all our prayers and that You are interested in everything that happens to us. My favorite team is playing today and I am very excited about it. I am very hopeful that they will win.

Help me to be calm so that no matter what happens, I may not forget my manners and my love for others. Help me to behave as I ought. Prevent my excitement from creating rivalries and animosity with others. May I be a good fan, encouraging and supporting my team without promoting violence or disrespect for the competition. Give me peace that I may enjoy this competition in a healthy way, as a good child of God. In the name of Christ. Amen.

My Friends

I Have Acted Like a Fool

SUGGESTED READING: 2 CORINTHIANS

12:11–13

———∽∞∾———

Lord of Peace, pardon my anger. Forgive me because I have acted poorly. I lost my cool; I felt offended. When I feel unfairly treated, much pain and anger awakens within me! I felt so offended that I reacted by saying words that I should not have—and now I am embarrassed just remembering them. Those whom I have helped so much and for whom I gave my life now treat me so unfairly.

Help me, Lord, to pardon them and to ask them for forgiveness for what I said. Grant that the sun not set on my anger. I know that in Christ I will find the strength to get over this. Jesus suffered for my sins so that I am for-given. Help me now to imitate His example, to accept this suffering for the good of others. Grant that my soul be healed so that my guilt will not fill me with regret. In Your name, Christ Jesus. Amen.

Prayer about a Conflict
between Two People

SUGGESTED READING: 1 SAMUEL 25:1–35

—⁂—

Heavenly Father, Lord of peace, I always appreciate that You have taught me how important and healthy it is to forgive those who have offended us, as well as to offer pardon to the repentant. You want me to be a vehicle for forgiveness, an ambassador of reconciliation, and a peacemaker for those who are in conflict. This job often overwhelms me, and I want to flee or take sides because being in the middle is challenging.

Lord, help me to carry Your message of peace into this situation and to those involved. Help me to soothe their anger, to listen to their bitterness and hatred, to placate their desires for vengeance, and to be willing to expose myself to personal risk so that peace might be planted. By living among us, Jesus acted as a mediator so that we might live in peace. May that spirit of sacrifice encourage me to do the same for these people whom I love so much and who have fought with each other. Bless my actions and words so that with patience and dedication I might be able to plant seeds of peace. In Christ's name. Amen.

I Spoke Ill of a Friend

SUGGESTED READING: PROVERBS 10:18–22

Lord of words, I am grateful for being able to talk with my friends. But sometimes I would rather be unable to speak so that I would not say mean and nasty things. I have offended a friend by saying things that I should not have. I think they were not even true, and even if they had been, they were not uplifting at all.

Lord, how could I have been so weak? How could I have lost control of my tongue? Lies, gossip, and slander are so sweet for a moment, but I feel terrible after telling them. Forgive me, Lord. Encourage me to fight for our friendship and to ask for forgiveness with sincere repentance. I think that this will teach me to talk less and to be more careful in what I say.

I am a sinner, a sinner with words. I am a sinner who has offended the ears and the heart of a friend. May Jesus' forgiveness restore my life and help me to seek my friend's forgiveness. In the name of Christ. Amen.

Friends Have Lied and Falsely Accused Me

SUGGESTED READING: PSALM 3

———∞∞∞———

Lord of righteousness, I feel so bad. I am over whelmed with feelings of vengeance and bitterness. I cannot concentrate or think clearly. I feel like I am the victim of some evil plan. People are saying things about me that are not true. I have been wounded deeply by their words. They blame me for things that are not my fault.

Help me, Lord. This is like a poison that fills my body with bitterness and violence. I have never felt this horrible before. I am beginning to understand what Jesus felt when He was judged, and I believe He can understand what I am feeling right now.

Give me patience and self control in great measure, so that I do not attempt to repay evil with evil. Give me faith to trust that You will justify me because vengeance is Yours, and You will show me Your mercy. But especially, give me peace in my heart to be able to withstand this suffering. I am falling apart. In Christ's name. Amen.

I Need to Ask for Forgiveness
SUGGESTED READING: MATTHEW 5:21–24

—∞∞∞—

Lord of reconciliation, thank You for forgiving my sins through Jesus Christ and teaching me the value of peace. You show me how to offer forgiveness to those around me. Today, Lord, I need Your help. Give me the humility and the courage to ask for forgiveness. I have offended my friend, and I am ashamed of what I have done. I have thought about it, and what I did was wrong. I gain no satisfaction by making excuses or blaming others. I am repentant, but I do not know how to ask for forgiveness.

Lord, make obedience to Your Word, the need for living in peace, the value of our friendship and of good relations matter more than my fears, shame, and guilt. Lord, guide my words and strengthen my knees so that I can ask for forgiveness. In Christ's name. Amen.

I Miss Someone and I Haven't Received Any Word

SUGGESTED READING: 2 TIMOTHY 4:9–13

—— ∞ ——

O Lord, thank You for Your everlasting friendship. You are always there, even when everyone else leaves. Thank You for Your comfort that is so real that I can feel Your presence in all the chaos of this world.

Lord, today I am missing a friend from whom I have not heard in a while. A strange sadness and melancholy cause me to feel a special need for a hug, a conversation, or the presence of another person. Iron sharpens iron, and, Lord, I need to be with my friend.

Sometimes it is good to be apart so that we can realize how much we love each other. Help me to look forward to our meeting again. Help me to seek a way to communicate with my friend, to share my affection, and to value the friendship that is so good for us. And if this is not possible, Lord, give me the joy of knowing that it is okay and that You made our paths cross so that we could share some good times. Thank You because, despite my melancholy, You are always there. Please allow us to see each other again soon. In the name of Christ. Amen.

I Have a Friend Who Is Far Away

SUGGESTED READING: 1 SAMUEL 20:18–42

L ord of the distances, every day I give thanks for having You near me and for being able to count on You as my friend. It does not matter how far up in the heavens or how remote a place I may be in, Your Spirit brings us together and keeps us close.

But there are distances that are not so easy to overcome. I have a friend who is far away, a great distance is between us. My friend is not just far away—I feel that our friendship is weakening and falling apart. Even though I try to keep it alive, I get the impression that it is not what it once was.

Help me, Lord, to accept these circumstances that I am going through. May I understand that it is not anyone's fault that this is happening; drifting apart is natural and it does not make sense to try to force things. Each one of us has a path to travel that You have laid out for us. Teach us to leave our friendship in Your care, and not to ruin it in a useless effort to stay in a time and place that have passed. Lord of all friends, care for us every day, so that on the day we meet again, everything may feel the same as ever. In Christ's name. Amen.

I Have a Friend Who Is Homosexual

SUGGESTED READING: 1 CORINTHIANS 6:9–11

Lord of mercy and truth, I am surprised to find out that my friend is homosexual. Nothing like this has ever happened to me. I ought to admit that I feel very confused about how to treat my friend now. I try to act like everything is fine, that I do not care, but the truth is that I am afraid.

I know that You do not approve this behavior and You condemn those who practice it. I also know that You forgive those who recognize their sin and believe in Jesus and You give them the chance to start a new life. So I am praying for my friend. Help me not to reject him (her) because we are all sinners and it is not good to discriminate. Help me to invite him (her) to meditate on his (her) behavior without condemning him (her). This way he (she) may find strength in the Holy Spirit to recognize his (her) sin and to benefit from forgiveness. Give him (her) new life, Lord.

I know that this isn't a small request and that it might not end up the way I want it to. Give me patience, wisdom, and love to act justly. May Christ be my protector and guide. In His name. Amen.

My Best Friend Has Died

SUGGESTED READING: JOB 2:11–13

⸺⸱⸺

Lord of comfort, my soul is aching. It is as if part of my own life has been ripped apart.

Thank You, Lord, for the time that my friend and I were able to enjoy together. Thank You for the good and bad times that we shared which have helped us to grow. This friend was like a sibling that I got to choose.

Lord, give me the comfort I need. Give me the silence of Your presence that gives calm to my soul in the most turbulent moments. Those around me share my pain, but many do not share the comfort I have. May I feel Your peace, so that I can offer it to others. Give me the peace that comes from knowing that as I say goodbye to my friend he (she) will no longer be. A part of my life has come to a close, but You are eternal and You always help me. Reaffirm the good times we enjoyed as friends. In the name of Jesus. Amen.

A Friend Has Heard the Gospel Today
SUGGESTED READING: ACTS 8:26–40

Creator of the faith, what a beautiful experience I have had today! Thank You for the opportunity to share the message of the Gospel with my friend. I had never thought it would happen like this, but I understand that Your times and Your ways are not like ours.

I saw the look on my friend's face, listening intently to the Bible's teachings. I have sensed his (her) repentance for having lived in sin and at odds with You. But I was able to share in his (her) joy in knowing that Jesus died for our sins to give us pardon and eternal life.

I want to thank You, Lord, because Your Holy Spirit has planted faith in my friend's heart and has renewed it. You have made him (her) Your child and given him (her) Your salvation. Protect him (her) from every evil and help him (her) to grow. Keep me from thinking that this is all due to my witness. Lead me to pray humbly for my friend and to walk with him (her) until he (she) feels secure in this new faith. I am so glad to be an instrument in this miracle of new life. In Christ's name, who also saved me. Amen.

I Have a Very Worldly Friend
SUGGESTED READING: GALATIANS 5:16–24

———

Lord of holiness, thank You for Your Holy Spirit, who has brought me to know the Gospel and to begin a new life. Thank You for Your Word that guides me so that I may live in holiness and leave behind the pursuits of this world.

I have a friend who does not seem to know that another way of life is possible. I am coming to You to pray for my friend, whose conduct as a believer leaves much to be desired. He (she) seems like a person of this world! It seems like he (she) does not recognize the power that he (she) has through the Holy Spirit to overcome his (her) weaknesses.

You have taught us that, if we see someone caught in sin, we should restore that person with a humble attitude because we also may be tempted. With this humility, I ask You, Lord, to help me to cause my friend to be rehabilitated and to challenge him (her) to use and enjoy this new life in a holy way. May my friend grow in faith and in the knowledge of Your will, so that he (she) may live in purity and sincerity. May we help and encourage one another to overcome evil with good. In Christ's name. Amen.

Prayer on Friendship Day

SUGGESTED READING: 1 SAMUEL 18:1–4

———∞∞∞———

L ord of good friends, thank You for being a friendly God. Thank You for Your sincerity and for being so giving. Thank You for giving Jesus' life in order to rescue us from our evil ways. Thank You for such a wonderful example of true friendship. Help me to be a friend like Jesus has been to me.

Lord, bless my friends on this day so that we remember the value of friendship. May sincere affection, healthy and constructive criticism, friendly embraces, and shared laughter never be lacking among us. May we give without holding back so that we may receive in the same measure. May this friendship that You have created among us cause us to grow.

Lord of friendship, teach us also to seek reconciliation and forgiveness, which is the source of faithfulness in good friendships. In the name of Christ, our best friend. Amen.

Prayer for a Reunion
with High School Friends

SUGGESTED READING: ACTS 20:17–38

—— ∞ ——

Lord of reunions, thank You for the friends that You placed around me as I was growing up so that we could help each other with the abilities that You gave to us. Thank You for the experiences we have shared, both the pleasant and the unpleasant ones. Help us to forgive the mistakes and disagreements that came between us. Allow us to remember the good times, the ones that inspire reunions and allow us to continue to grow.

The challenges of life, our families, and other affairs have distanced us and taken us in different directions. Today, You allow us to reunite and to see where our paths have led. Allow us to praise Your greatness and love through this encounter. May we enjoy this friendship that remains alive through time and distance. In the name of Christ. Amen.

I Have a Friend Who Is Having Legal Problems

SUGGESTED READINGS: ROMANS 13:1–5;
1 PETER 3:13–17

—⊷∞⊶—

Lord of law and order, I pray for a friend who is having problems with the law. My friend has received various notices for having broken the laws of our land. His (her) guilt and fear have caused my friend to hide from the authorities and to flee from justice. Help my friend to understand the importance of obeying authority, for it has been established by You for the common good and for the maintaining of order. If the accusations are unjust, give my friend the strength and patience to withstand the injustice, demonstrating the hope that is in his (her) heart.

Father of justice, teach us to live in truth and in justice. Guide the judges with Your wisdom to impart justice with equity; cause those who enforce the law to be respectful of the detained. Aid those who have broken the law to recognize their error and negligence. Give them Your forgiveness, so that they can renew their lives and be rehabilitated to live in accordance with Your will through the strength of Your Spirit. In the name of Jesus Christ. Amen.

I Am Worried about a Friend

SUGGESTED READING: MATTHEW 8:14–17

⸺◦◦◦⸺

Heavenly Father, Lord of all friends, I am very worried about a friend who is going through a really hard time. We are far apart, and my friend needs me. Be with him (her) and lend Your strength so that he (she) can endure these hardships and find creative solutions.

Give me the right words to communicate comfort and strength. May the friendship that we share be strengthened during this difficult time. Help me to offer comfort and respite by providing the small things that my friend needs. May his (her) worries be mine as well. May what Jesus did for me when He saw me suffering motivate me to help my friend and to sympathize in a merciful way. Lord, may You and I together be with him (her) despite the distance between us while we await a solution to this problem that has affected him (her) so much. In the name of Jesus, my best friend. Amen.

For a Friend Who Has Fallen into Sin

SUGGESTED READING: GALATIANS 6:1–5

Lord of compassion, I am very upset because a good friend of mine has fallen into sin. It is hard for me to believe it. I feel cheated and angry, and want to punish him (her) for his (her) behavior. But I believe that that is not right. You have made us brothers (sisters) in the faith, and I always thought these things would not happen in our lives.

You want us to help carry each other's burdens. May we also exhort each other with humility because we are all capable of falling into sin. Help me to speak with him (her) in mercy and love so that he (she) might see his (her) sin and repent, trusting in Your forgiveness. Together may we remember Your great love for us and our vulnerability in the face of sin that leads to destruction. May the friendship You have knit between us motivate me to treat my friend with patience and great forgiveness. May Christ's example and His love for me guide my actions in accordance to Your will. In the name of Jesus Christ. Amen.

My World

Prayer for the Fruits of the Earth

SUGGESTED READING: PSALM 107:33–38

———∞———

Lord of the fruit of the fields and of the harvest, thank You for the silent and imperceptible power that blesses our work here on the earth. Whether we are asleep or awake, You make the trees and plants around grow and produce.

Lord, thank You for the wind and the insects and birds that You send to make the flowers bountiful. Thank You for all the fruits that our trees and plants produce. Help us to care for them so they develop, grow, and mature as one of the blessings of Your wonderful creation. Teach us to be grateful for this harvest and to share the fruits of love and justice through good deeds. May the fruits that You produce in us through Your Holy Spirit of love, faithfulness, patience, and joy sprout and grow in us, just like the fruits of the earth. Through this growth, the souls of others may be fed with the same faith that we have. And on the day of harvest, may we praise Your name because of Your love. In Christ's name. Amen.

MY WORLD

Prayer for Communications and Media
SUGGESTED READING: MATTHEW 12:35–37

⌘

Lord of communication, thank You for helping us to express ourselves with one another and to share our opinions and feelings in various ways. Thank You for those who work to promote communication and provide information for all people because they help to develop our community. Bless all the media that seek the well-being of people and that work with valor and good will to share their message accurately and responsibly.

Protect from all harm those whose work puts them in danger. Help them to ask intelligent questions and to be wise in their commentaries. Give them the ability they need to carry out their work well and speak with precision. Help them to guard their tongues so that they may not speak more than is necessary. May they generate trust and not cause confusion, bring respect rather than irreverence, and breed love rather than animosity. Through Christ, the Holy Word. Amen.

Prayer for Sun and Rain

SUGGESTED READING: PSALM 65:9–13

———— ∞ ————

Lord of the climates, thank You for the sun. Because of its heat and light our plans and trees grow, our fruits mature, and our life thrives. Thank You also for the rain, for the water that quenches the thirst of all living beings and nourishes the plants that nourish us.

Teach us to be grateful for the climate every day and to remember Your promises of care and provision for all humanity. Only in this way can we live without unnecessary worries and cares. Teach us to be grateful for the sunny days and the rainy ones and also for the wind, the cold, and the heat. May we learn that every type of weather has a reason. Father of the heavens, motivate us to work to maintain the laws of nature by adapting to them instead of modifying them for our own convenience. In the name of Christ, Lord of heaven and earth. Amen.

Prayer for Art

SUGGESTED READING: ECCLESIASTES 3:11–13

———— ∞ ————

God of all beauty, thank You for the works of art that we are able to admire. Thank You because You have placed an aesthetic sensibility in us and because there are people who labor to create works that inspire the admiration of art. Heavenly Father, Lord of full and perfect beauty, allow us to consider Your majesty through Your Spirit and through the small things that You place all around us.

Lord, bless those who work to promote the arts. Give them creativity, freedom, and patience to express their best sentiments, which You have inspired in them through their artwork. May this admiration inspire people to be thankful for the life that You give them and to work for lasting worth. Cause each object, no matter how small it may be, to serve Your glory and the well-being of neighbors. In the name of Jesus Christ, the primary inspiration of all art. Amen.

Prayer for Music

SUGGESTED READING: PSALM 150

—∞∞∞—

Lord of music and praise, thank You that we can express our feelings with voices and sounds. Thank You for the instruments that we can create to motivate ourselves and to accompany us in our praise and relaxation. Thank You for being a God who rejoices in the creativity of a new and joyful song.

Help us to accept the different musical tastes that exist in our world. Guide us so that we may take advantage of them to raise praises to You and to motivate our gratitude. Teach us to be respectful of the authors and composers of each musical piece and to encourage those who work in creating new songs and praises. May routine not limit our adoration. Thank You for the gifts that You have given us. Let us take advantage of the talents You've placed in us in order to give glory to Your name wherever we may use them. Help us to receive criticism that will help us to improve. Thank You, Lord, in Jesus Christ, the reason for our songs. Amen.

Prayer for a Good Planting and for a Good Harvest

SUGGESTED READING: PSALM 126:5–6

L ord of the fields and of the sown earth, thank You because we have been able to sow this year. We are very hopeful every time we plant seeds in the ground. Although we do our work willingly and as well as we can, we know that the harvest depends on Your good and sovereign will. We know that, although we sow with tears and sacrifice, Your blessing will fill us with joy.

Guide us so that we may also sow Your Gospel with the same hope and faith, trusting in the invisible and powerful action of Your Holy Spirit. Bless this work so that it may produce and fill our faces with joy and smiles. When we gather the harvest, may we celebrate with You the wonderful miracle of life that flows out of death. Strengthen our faith and hope with prayer and with the reading of Your Word. May we never despair or feel guilty when facing the difficulties that may arise. In the name of the Lord of the harvest. Amen.

Prayer for a Move
SUGGESTED READING: MATTHEW 2:13–15

Heavenly Father, Lord of change, we are moving and we are filled with memories and mixed feelings—joys and sorrows, fears and expectations. Help us in these days of confusion so that our mind remains clear and attentive to our responsibilities. Help us to say goodbye and bring healing to the relationships that You have allowed us to create and to enjoy in this place. This way we can create new ties and friendships in the place we are going.

Thank You for all that we have been able to do and enjoy in this time and place that we are leaving behind. Cause the doors of our hearts to always remain open. Thank You for all the affection that we have received from our neighbors, friends, and church family. Some we may never see again. Keep us healthy and care for each one of us, because time and space are nothing to You. Bless us in our new home. Give us patience as we get settled into it, unpack, and enjoy the new space we will inhabit. May Your presence be as real in our new home as it has always been here. With You we can face every change that comes our way. In the name of Christ, the traveling God. Amen.

In an Emergency

SUGGESTED READING: GENESIS 19:12–26

───── ∞ ─────

God of speed and urgency, of patience and of wisdom, I ask that the Holy Spirit carry me in His arms during this emergency situation. There is not much time to think and we must make important decisions. Give us wisdom to act according to Your will. Take away our fear and despair.

Lord, also give us the strength we need to face this emergency. May this situation remind us that there are times we must act quickly, so our faith must be ready. In times of trial You always provide the ability to overcome the difficulties. I know I may make mistakes because of being in a rush. Soothe my spirit; give me hands that are willing to help my neighbor. May I be aware of Your presence and company. Help me to stay awake and alert. In the name of Christ. Amen.

My Family

I Want a Partner

SUGGESTED READING: GENESIS 24

Father of love, who sympathized with Adam's loneliness and provided a companion for him, help me also to find my mate. I do not know how or where to find him (her). Send Your angels to accompany me so that I may spend time in the right places. In Christ You promised that everyone who seeks with faith will find. Help me to keep my eyes open to the possibilities that present themselves and to not be afraid to ask. Give me courage to overcome my fears and trust that You will guide me to find the person that You have for me.

May prayer be my constant companion right now. I want to make a good decision, a choice guided by love. Thank You for these deep and wonderful feelings that You have placed in my life. By sharing them, cause me to grow as a person and especially to praise You for the possibility of sharing love. In Christ's name. Amen.

I am Having Doubts about Choosing My Spouse

SUGGESTED READING: 1 CORINTHIANS 13:4–7

⸺◦⸺

Lord of affection, thank You for allowing me to meet my partner. Thank You for making our paths cross and because we have shared this time together. But sometimes I have doubts. I think I may have made the wrong choice. Some actions and feelings, some irritations and thoughts make me want to end this relationship. I do not know what to do.

Guide me with Your Holy Spirit. He knows me better than I know myself. Let Your Word guide me toward knowledge of what love is. Give me the courage and the humility to talk about these doubts and uncertainties with my partner. Teach me to be sincere and to take advantage of this time to get to know each other better. May I accept that in a relationship things are not always harmonious. I want to learn to be patient, to tell the truth, and to seek justice. May I learn to support, to hope and to believe. I will be open, Lord, to having You show me the way. In Christ's name. Amen.

Someone in My Family Is Sick

SUGGESTED READING: MARK 5:21–24; 35–43

———∞∞∞———

Lord of health, thank You for being with us in this difficult time. The whole family is worried about this illness, and we are troubled and anxious because we don't know how the situation will work out. So we come to You; we know You are the one who directs our lives and that nothing happens without Your approval.

Help us, Lord, to submit to Your will, to bear with one another, and to encourage each other instead of stirring up guilt and pointing blame. Give us patience and a good disposition with the doctors. Help us to have the necessary discipline to adhere to the medication the schedule. Guide us with Your wisdom so that we can organize cooperatively in order to attend to the needs of the patient. But above all, help us in our faith and hope so that we may trust in Your power to cure. Prevent our prayer from ceasing because it is so good for us. Just as the Lord Jesus cured so many ills, Lord, cure our loved one with Your powerful hand. We ask this in His name. Amen.

Kids These Days!

SUGGESTED READING: MATTHEW 19:16–22

———— ✺ ————

Lord of all generations, You are a wonderful God who does not discriminate between people. You care for each of us equally, whether children, the elderly, teens, adults, women or men. Thank You for being with our youth.

Give us ears to hear their uncertainties and wisdom so that we do not mislead them or hinder their spiritual growth. Give us tolerance to withstand their pride and the right words to make them consider that life is not as simple as they see it. Give us the words to invite them to commit themselves to high ideals, especially in their faith in Jesus Christ. May we motivate them to look beyond what they always see and to renounce the worthless treasures of this world in favor of those that await us in heaven. We ask this in the name of Christ, a youth with His feet firmly planted on the earth and eyes always fixed on heaven, who loved us until the end. Amen.

Help Me with These Children!

SUGGESTED READING: MATTHEW 19:16–22

Lord of the children, You understand the little ones more than we can even imagine. You sent Your Son Jesus to be a child. You reprimanded the disciples for casting children aside and despising them. Thus, Lord, I beg You to help me with these kids. I want to give them the same treatment that You give them; I want to love them with my whole heart, seek them when they are straying, correct them, slow them down, and steer them on the right path.

There are days, Lord, when this blessing that You have given to me becomes a heavy burden, to the point that I become frustrated. I am supposed to teach so many things: to obey and respect, but also to eat and to walk; to get along well with others, and also to overcome the pain of loss. Lord, give me wisdom from heaven, which will teach me to weather it all without losing my senses and to use my abilities without giving up. Grant that my concern for children be like Yours, and that I might be able to understand and believe that You are helping me in this beautiful task that You have given me by giving me these children. Thank You, Lord! In the name of Jesus, the best friend of my children. Amen.

My Father Is an Alcoholic
SUGGESTED READING: GENESIS 9:20–27

———∞∞∞———

Heavenly Father, Lord of the sick and dependent, thank You for always protecting my father during those times that he has lost control of his senses. I regret that this is happening and I pray that You would help me to find a way to overcome it. I feel ashamed of his behavior and of his drunkenness. I vacillate between wanting to mock him and feeling indifferent, being fearful and becoming desperate. I wish I could get away from all this, but I understand that You want me to help.

Lord, I ask You to fill me with the respect for him that he deserves as my father and as a person. May I find the best way to act towards him, forgiving his offenses against me and the rest of the family. This is a very difficult situation to resolve, but I trust that You will guide us with patience, love, and good will to seek the solution together that will help us to overcome this illness. Heavenly Father, good Father, protect him while we look for the blanket to cover his nakedness. In the name of Christ, who has freed so many from the snares of sin and who is guiding and strengthening us even now. Amen.

For My Birthday

SUGGESTED READING: PROVERBS 4:10–13

⸻

L ord of our years, thank You because we can celebrate this birthday and for the life that You've granted me. Thank You because I can remember Your salvation through Jesus and for the special presence of Your Spirit in my heart. You are a wonderful God, who is always beside me in every circumstance—in the past, in the present and in the future.

I especially ask for Your presence in this special day of celebration. Fill this place and our hearts with Your joy, with good humor, and lots of fun. Allow brotherly love to be reflected in the smiles and affection. May we forgive each other's mistakes and sins so that the patience and tolerance we have learned from Jesus may flourish. May the best gift be the time we can spend celebrating together at this party. And may this new year of life be a reason to be grateful for Your great love that motivates us to live more fully in our years to come. In Jesus, who always brought joy to all celebrations. Amen.

A Wedding Anniversary
SUGGESTED READING: JOHN 2:1–11

---∞∞∞---

Lord of marriage, thank You for this wedding anniversary that You have allowed us to celebrate. Thank You for guiding us and teaching us with Your Word so that we might learn the wonderful art of loving, forgiving, and submitting to one another. Without Your presence and aid, it would be difficult to accept our mistakes, to put up with one another, and to enjoy each other. Thank You, Lord, for the example that You have given us in Christ and His love for the Church.

Getting to this day has been a fun adventure and a great challenge. Together with You, we have learned how wonderful marriage is, created by You for our delight and our growth. Encourage us when we fail; motivate us to reconcile and to live in peace when we grow apart, and keep us strong in the faith that unites us with a love stronger than death. Lord of our lives, thank You for every day we share, and turn our water into wine. In Christ's name. Amen.

My Parents Are Not Believers

SUGGESTED READING: ROMANS 9:1–5

—⊗⊗⊗—

Heavenly Father, giver of faith, thank You for the Holy Spirit who has planted the seeds of faith in my life. It was He who made me see my sinfulness and believe that Jesus died and rose for me. This has motivated me to want others to enjoy this blessing, including my family and especially my parents.

You know how my parents are and all the care and love that they have always shown me. You know my affection for them and that I would give anything necessary so that they might believe. But they are tied to other things that they believe bring them security and life. I do not know how to face this situation without creating problems. I am afraid of a lot of things, but the greatest is that I have not done anything to help them believe. Lord, I want You to give me the courage that I need to communicate the Gospel to them; to open my heart before them with all respect, and to trust in the action of Your Holy Spirit in their lives. I love my parents, Lord, but the greatest blessing for me would be that they would also be part of the family of faith. In the name of Christ, who experienced something similar in His own family. Amen.

For Rebellious Children

———— ❧ ————

Loving Father, God of patience and wisdom, my heart aches. I feel so much shame because of my children's behavior. I have taught them as best I could. I have not left them in need of anything. I have also taught them Your commandments. I have brought them to meet You and I have prayed thousands of times for their health and growth.

Lord, my children have become rebellious. They do things they should not and they are not ashamed of their sins. Everyone knows about this and they look at me with pity, derision, and even with anger.

Lord, help me because I am desperate! These are my children, and I love them. I want the best for them, but they do not listen to me anymore. They treat me with disrespect. I have lost my authority! Forgive me all the mistakes I have made with them, because I cannot stand the guilt I feel about all of this. Give me patience to stay in the fight for their rehabilitation, and grant me much wisdom to take the right steps in order to help them. Lord, how many times have I acted the same way with You? Help me to follow Your example of a loving and merciful father. Help me to not lose my hope in You. In the name of Christ Jesus. Amen.

Prayer for My Mother

SUGGESTED READING: LUKE 1:26-31

⎯⎯∞⎯⎯

Lord of the family, in Your great power and grace You give women the privilege and joy of carrying a child, and in the wonderful mystery of Your creative power, You show Your greatness and love for the entire human race. Thank You for the mother who carried me and cared for me from the very first days of my life. Thank You for her tenderness, her kisses, and her constant care for my health and well-being.

Bless her days so that she may get all she deserves for her efforts. Forgive her mistakes so that she does not suffer for the things that she tried to do in a different way that did not work out well. Give her Your presence and comfort so that she would enjoy the satisfaction of having been a mother, a blessing that comes from heaven, from the God of life.

Lord, bless the mother that You have given me and bless the woman You created. Give her strength to enjoy her children. In Christ's name, the Savior who always cared about His mother. Amen.

Prayer for My Father

SUGGESTED READING:

MATTHEW 2:13–15, 19–23

———◆◆◆———

L ord of the family, thank You for giving me a father who watches over me in this life, a father who seeks to follow Your will and to lead me in the right direction. Guide him, Lord, so that he may live according to Your will and listen to Your voice. Lead him and the whole family in the path that You have laid out.

Lord, give him the wisdom to govern the house and to lead us according to Your teaching; the strength to establish the necessary limits for our discipline; and the love to lead us in our projects and challenges. Lord, I thank You because I can count on my Dad. Teach me to forgive his mistakes and to give him the respect he deserves. Teach us to get along and to understand each other, just as You got along with Your Son here on earth. In the name of Jesus. Amen.

Prayer for Grandparents
SUGGESTED READING: 2 TIMOTHY 1:3–5

———

God and Father of all generations, thank You for my grandparents, for their example in life and especially for their testimony of faith. Thank You because they have known how to share the essential teachings of Your Word consistently and faithfully with us; they taught us to respect You and to seek You in times of need and to praise You and thank You in times of blessing and prosperity.

Lord, bless my grandparents. Accompany them now while their strength and abilities are beginning to wane so that their spiritual strength continues with integrity. Bless their words so that they might be wise, imparting experiences of a life lived in accordance with Your will. Protect them from all misfortune and danger so that we may enjoy this wonderful time together that You have given us during different stages of our lives. In the name of Christ Jesus. Amen.

Prayer for My Baby

SUGGESTED READING: EXODUS 2:1–10

Heavenly Father, guardian of our children. I thank You for this beautiful baby that You have given me. Thank You for his (her) tenderness and warmth, because even in the absence of language and movement, we feel each other's mutually-enriching vitality. His (her) presence has changed my life and filled it with happiness and with a new level of responsibility. It is my duty to protect him (her) and to help him (her) to grow.

Lord, I am seeking Your help with this difficult task. I have many fears and there are dangers that I must protect him (her) from. I constantly worry about his (her) health, growth, and times of silence. However, I know I can count on You, and I ought not obsess. You have given me this child and You will help me to raise him (her) by giving me the strength, the ability, and the wisdom to protect him (her) from all harm. Lord, may You be the basket that protects my child in this river. In the name of Jesus Christ. Amen.

A Loved One Has Died
SUGGESTED READING: JOHN 11:28–36

⊶⊷

Lord of the beginning and of the end, You under
stand our sufferings and You comfort us in
moments of pain. I feel that I have lost my strength
because of the sadness in my heart. I am left speechless
in the face of the reality that I am living. I wish this
were a dream, but unfortunately it is real.

Help me in this time of intense pain. Strengthen my
faith in Your promises of resurrection and eternal life.
Today more than ever I need to believe and to have hope
so that this sadness will not harm me. Remove all guilt
from my heart and fill me with peace. Death does exist,
and it is unpleasant and painful. We cannot avoid it. But
You are the source of comfort during this painful time.

Lord, give me words and actions that will comfort my
family, and, like Jesus, may I console the suffering with
words of eternal life. In the name of Jesus Christ. Amen.

I am Having Trouble in My Marriage
SUGGESTED READING: 1 CORINTHIANS 7:1–6

Heavenly Father, You created us male and female so that we might be content together. Thank You for allowing us to meet and to fall in love; thank You for being with us and for protecting us from many dangers and allowing us to marry—to pledge our love and mutual help forever.

We pray for our marriage. Little by little, small matters have come between us, creating disagreements that continue to escalate. Lord, help us to remember our marriage commitment; keep us from growing distant; help us to forgive each other's mistakes. We lack the strength and enthusiasm that we had before. Father God, You have promised Your blessing, aid, and care. We need You today more than ever. There is some unknown problem that is threatening our marriage, and we do not know how to fight against it. Give us wisdom to identify it; grant us patience to forgive each other; and through Your Word help us to imitate the love that Christ had for the Church as the model for our married life. In the name of Jesus Christ. Amen.

My Daughter Is a Woman Now

SUGGESTED READING: MATTHEW 25:1–13

—∞∞∞—

L ord of life and growth, thank You for protecting my little girl. She is all grown up now. How wonderful is Your creation! I am grateful that she has developed well physically, and today for the first time she is showing evidence that she can be a mother someday. This makes me so happy, but it also fills me with worry and fear.

Help her to accept the challenges of this new phase in her life. May she embrace her womanhood despite the pain, the cycles, and the complications. I want my daughter to enjoy her adolescence and young adulthood, and I pray especially that she might make good choices; may she carry enough oil in her lamp to maintain the flame of her faith. Lord, give us the ability and the wisdom to accompany her while she grows up. May we pray for her and help her to discern right from wrong.

Lord, bless her and send Your angels to protect her so that she may be a happy and responsible young woman. We ask this in Jesus' name. Amen.

Prayer for My Sister

SUGGESTED READING: LUKE 10:38–42

⎯⎯⎯∞⎯⎯⎯

Heavenly Father, Lord of brotherhood and sisterhood, thank You for giving me a sister with whom I have shared many good times and some more difficult ones, too. Thank You for all that she has contributed to my growth as a person. Thank You for the personality You have given her that, although sometimes it is hard for me to accept, has allowed me to learn to relate to people who are different from me.

Sometimes she does not choose her priorities very well and she becomes distracted by a thousand worries. Other times her faith is more firm and practical than mine. Lord, give her the opportunity to find the happiness that she desires. Bless her with Your company and protection to make her healthy so that she might be able to serve You always. Help us to understand each other and to strengthen our friendship. This way, in addition to the ties and blood and affection that bind us together, we may also be united by the bond of faith. If life's circumstances lead us in separate directions, help us to always remember how important it is to maintain good relationships with our siblings. In the name of Jesus Christ. Amen.

Prayer for My Godchild

SUGGESTED READING: GENESIS 18:23–33

———— ∞ ————

Lord of choices, thank You for this godchild that You have given me. Thank You for allowing me to share the beautiful task of raising him (her) in the faith with his (her) parents. Help me to be responsible in the promise and commitment that I have made before Your altar. I beg You to protect and care for his (her) life.

Sometimes he (she) is not even aware of the evil that surrounds him (her). He (she) is a bit selfish and does not worry about living in accordance with Your will. Forgive him (her), Lord. Perhaps his (her) parents cannot spend any more time and energy with him (her) than they do now. Maybe we have not known how to share our faith in You with him (her). But to me he (she) is like my own child, and I want to lead him (her) in Your truth. I ask You to give me wise words that reach his (her) heart. Forgive his (her) carelessness and give him (her) a chance to rebuild his (her) life. Lord, care for him (her) by Your grace so that this difficult period might pass and that together we might grow as a family. In Christ's name. Amen.

My Brother Is Spending Time with Bad Influences

SUGGESTED READING: PROVERBS 1:8–19

———— ❦ ————

Heavenly Father, Lord of the holy life, I am very worried about my brother. He is spending time with friends who I do not think are good for him. Their behavior is strange, their words are ingenuous and full of evil intent; they are up to no good.

I have talked with him and he got mad at me. He treated me like a goody two shoes and a busybody. Despite the pain that his rejection has caused, Lord, I believe that he will need Your help to realize that he is more vulnerable than he realizes. I do not want him to live in a bubble or to be alienated from everyone, but I want him to pay attention to what he is doing and to recognize that he could fall into sin.

Lord, protect him. Do not lead him into temptation, and deliver him from the evil that is threatening him. May Your Holy Spirit rehabilitate him and give him the strength to triumph over evil. Perhaps You have a special purpose for the friendships that he has now; if that is the case, then may he influence them with the values that he has learned. And if that is not the case, may he flee before he falls into sin. I ask this in the name of Christ, who taught us to be as innocent as doves and as wise as serpents. Amen.

My Loved One Is Sick with Cancer
SUGGESTED READING: ACTS 28:1–10

———

Lord of health, I seek You today because I am distressed, along with all my family, because our loved one is suffering from cancer. Lord, I know that it is an illness that can be cured, but it is also serious and dangerous. The news has caused us great anguish and we do not know what to do. Just the word itself scares us and makes us focus on death.

But we know You are a powerful and almighty God who has authority over everything in earth and in heaven. You are the Lord of all time and of our lives. We pray on behalf of our loved one, for whom we feel such great affection. Cure him (her) of this illness so that we all may be well. Help him (her) in this difficult time, during all the complicated tests and treatments, so that he (she) may have the strength of body and spirit to persevere. Hear our prayers, and may they be a witness of our faith in You and of Your greatness and mercy that You show to Your children. In the name of Jesus. Amen.

My Relatives Are Coming to Visit
SUGGESTED READING: LUKE 1:39–45

———— ∞∞∞ ————

Lord of all joy, thank You for the joy of being reunited with my family. Thank You for the familial bonds that unite us and mutually enrich our lives. It is a blessing to be able to share time together with them once again.

Bless this visit so that we may praise Your name. Help to us to recognize Your goodness, which You allow us to share in our lives together. Protect us from all harm and danger. Give us good weather and ample time to talk and to catch up. May we be able to forgive each other's mistakes and to encourage one another to grow as people and as Your children. May the visit be as pleasant as Mary's visit to her cousin Elizabeth's house; this way we will be filled with joy and satisfaction because of the wonders that You have done in each of our lives. Remain with us so that our joy may be full. In Christ's name. Amen.

We Are Not Able to Have Children

SUGGESTED READING: 1 SAMUEL 1:1–20

———

Heavenly Father, Creator of all children, we humbly bow before Your throne in recognition of the fact that, despite all our plans and dreams, if You do not build a house, the hands that build it work in vain. If You do not bless the seed, the laborer works in vain. In our case, Lord, our desires for a child are empty if You do not accompany our wishes with Your blessing.

We do not know why we cannot have children; we have been trying for a long time. Still, You've never denied Your blessing to all those men and women who sought You and trusted in You. We believe that You know our suffering in this area. Help us to accept that Your time is not the same as our time and that You may be trying to teach us something as a couple.

Beyond everything that we do not understand, we ask You to bless us with a child. May our love and our faith in You increase while we wait. You are the Lord of life who blesses marriages to be fruitful and multiply. Grant us this blessing so that we may praise Your name and come to know, once again, that You are the only God in the whole earth. In Christ's name. Amen.

I Am Nostalgic before My Wedding

SUGGESTED READING: RUTH 1:15–18

———— ∞∞∞ ————

Lord of all happiness, thank You for the partner that You have given me; thank You that I have been able to grow in love and that You have inspired me to get engaged and to form a new family. We are convinced that You want us to be together for our entire lives and to share all that we have and are.

Nostalgia has been awakened in my heart. To create a new family, I have to leave the family I already have. You invite us to leave our father and our mother and to be united to our spouse so that we may live as one flesh. I had never thought about the profound nature of that idea until today when I began having doubts.

Help me to set good priorities in my treatment toward my partner and my parents. I must leave this house with all its warmth, and even though I will have better homes, this change is painful for me. Give me the determination I need to be able to view this as a benefit for everyone instead of a loss. Lord, teach me to value people so that I may appreciate my parents and siblings and the time we have shared together; in this way I will learn to live in a new phase in life, a time of blessing and of new roles that will help us to grow and improve. In the name of Christ. Amen.

Pitfalls of Being in a Relationship
SUGGESTED READING: 2 SAMUEL 13:1–19

———

Lord of purity and chastity, I am in a new relationship and I cannot stop thinking about the desires that have been awakened within me. There is a passion within me that constantly seeks the hugs, kisses, and caresses of this person above all else. It is something pleasant, but I feel fearful that these desires will increase and that I will not be able to appreciate any other aspects of this relationship.

Lord, that is why I want You to help me to be wise. Help me to control my passions and desires. May we establish healthy limits in this relationship so that the sexual aspect does not become all-consuming. Protect us, Lord, from falling into temptation. Lord, help me to talk about these matters with someone who can help me so that I do not become the victim of pressure or of vain desires. I am ashamed, Lord, but I prefer that our relationship not end badly. I ask this in Christ, the Lord of all strength and wisdom. Amen.

My Son Is Growing Up

SUGGESTED READING: LUKE 2:51-52

———— ⨎ ————

Lord of everyday things, thank You for caring for my son—he is growing up now. His clothes do not fit anymore, and his height and weight are no longer those of a child. He is big—we cannot carry him to his bedroom anymore—and although we have always longed for the arrival of this day, now that he is growing up we are having some fears that we do not know how to handle. His feelings and thoughts are changing, and his reasoning leaves us with our mouths hanging open.

Lord, guide us in this time of change so that we might understand him and steer his energies. May he grow also in Your grace and in Your love, in deeper knowledge of Your everlasting truth. Help us to grow also in the ways that we treat him. May we be flexible in some matters and strict in others, and we ask You especially to make us wise enough to know the difference. May we know how to forgive now more than ever, and may our son find us, his parents, to be people he can trust. Make him to grow up physically, emotionally, and spiritually healthy and strong. We ask this in the name of Jesus Christ. Amen.

My Child's Confirmation Day

SUGGESTED READING: MATTHEW 16:13–20

꧁꧂

Heavenly Father, who ignites and inspires our faith, thank You for having touched my child's life, that he (she) has gotten to know You better through Your Word and by the action of the Holy Spirit. I have prayed so much for him (her) and guided him (her) through many uncertainties! However, I always knew that only Your Holy Spirit could knock on the door of his (her) heart and enter.

He (she) has decided to do his (her) confession of faith in front of the church family. He (she) believes in his (her) heart and confesses with his (her) mouth in order to be saved. It will be a very special moment for him (her) and very meaningful for us. He (she) will recognize his (her) sinfulness and confess his (her) faith in Jesus. He (she) will promise fidelity and service to Your kingdom.

May his (her) confession of faith be sincere and aware that the Holy Spirit has revealed this marvelous grace to him (her). Protect him (her) from every evil and help him (her) to continue to grow in faith. In the name of Christ, in whom we believe and confess that we may be saved. Amen.

My Child Is Sick

SUGGESTED READING: 2 KINGS 4:8–37

———∞∞———

God of health, I feel very afraid because my child is sick. You have blessed me with his (her) life and together, day by day, we enjoy many things. But now he (she) is sick and I do not know what to do. I have been to the doctor and, although that calmed me down some, I am still worried. So I come before Your presence to ask for Your strength; I need it so that my hope and energies do not wane.

Protect my child from every evil and, by Your great power, cure his (her) illness. I know that You can do a miracle or strengthen him (her) with Your presence until he (she) recovers, bit by bit. Give him (her) patience to remain in bed and creativity to stay entertained while he (she) is getting well. And help me to share my faith, hope, affection, and prayers with him (her) so that I can be an encouragement. In Christ's name, the healer of our souls and our powerful Lord. Amen.

My Baby Was Born Sick

SUGGESTED READING: 2 SAMUEL 12:15–23

———∞———

Lord of miracles, the fear we feel in this moment is indescribable. We waited and hoped for months for this day to arrive to celebrate the birth of this baby, and now that he (she) has arrived, we are overwhelmed with grief because he (she) was born with health problems. Lord, our baby is very ill, and even though the doctors are doing all they can to help him (her) through, everything really depends on Your mercy and grace.

Our baby is so small and cannot fight for his (her) own life. We feel powerless. Be with us, Lord, in this moment of great sadness and uncertainty. We know that You are the one who gives life and who takes it away. We know Your will is best, although our firm hope is that our baby will survive. We beg You, though our faith is weak, that You will heal, save, and protect him (her). Guide the doctors so that they may find the best way to heal our child. In the name of Christ, our Savior. Amen.

Getting Along with My Brother

SUGGESTED READING: MATTHEW 5:21–26

———— ∞ ————

Creator of the bonds of kinship and of faith, thank You for the family You have given me. Thank You for my parents and my brothers and sisters, even though sometimes it is hard for me to get along with them. You know that I am recently having an especially hard time relating to my brother. Our relationship has not been too good. Actually, we have said some harsh words to each other and we have not made up. I feel bad because I have pretended that our conflict wasn't important. You want us to love and respect each other. This is Your command for us as brothers, and especially as brothers in the faith. Lord, I want to ask for Your help. It is hard for me to face this situation and to speak with my brother. I am afraid our animosity may increase even more. Prepare my heart for peace. Help me to swallow my pride and to be obedient to Your command to offer forgiveness. I know that I can do it, although I may suffer mockery or unjust treatment because of it. Even though I seem like the loser, I prefer to lose a tiny battle than to lose my brother. Lord, guide me and teach me to live in peace. In the name of Christ. Amen.

Prayer before Meals

SUGGESTED READING: 1 CORINTHIANS 10:25–31

———— ᧞᧞᧞᧞ ————

Creator and Sustainer of life—the earth is Yours and everything in it. We give You thanks for this food we are going to share because it comes from Your hand. Be our guest of honor at this table so that Your presence may bring harmony. Whether we eat or drink, we want to do everything for Your glory.

We thank You for Your great love for us, which You demonstrate in the fruits of the earth that You provide so that we may live. Teach us to share, to be responsible in eating and drinking so that what we consume may be a benefit to our bodies. May Your presence be what inspires us the most to enjoy time sharing this food. In Christ's name, who gave thanks and blessed the bread for the feeding of His people. Amen.

Prayer on My Father's Birthday

SUGGESTED READING: EZEKIEL 18:1–20

Lord of fatherhood, Jesus' example as a son is the inspiration for all Your children who desire to live in good relationships with their parents. Thank You for my Dad's birthday. Thank You for his love and care, for his disposition and his good will. I am grateful that we could be close, to learn together, to forgive each other, and to accept our differences.

Bless him today so that he might enjoy the successes he has achieved. May he especially enjoy the children You have given him, who are blessings that come from You. Lord, give him wisdom to continue being a good father in order that he may grow in virtue and ability and recognize his mistakes and weaknesses. Strengthen him to face the new challenges of these changing times, and give him plenty of patience. May the strength of the Holy Spirit allow him to carry out his role as father with great tenderness and creativity. In the name of Christ Jesus, the loving son of the heavenly Father. Amen.

Prayer for My Nephews and Nieces

SUGGESTED READING: GENESIS 13:2–12

Lord of the family, thank You for the relatives and the extended family that You have given me. Thank You for their affection, support, and also for the challenges that they bring. Thank You for my nephews and nieces, for the children of my siblings and in-laws. Allow me to develop good relationships with them because they are like my own siblings and children.

Help me to offer my support in every way that helps their physical and spiritual well-being. Inspire me to remember them in my prayers so that You would be present in their lives and protect them from every evil. Bless them in their decisions so that life would go well for them. Motivate us to teach our children to be respectful and to care about the well-being of their cousins, whether they are nearby or far away. Allow this relationship be a testimony of the love that unites us and a model of the care that You've shown us as our Father. May the ties of love and family that You have given to us be like a safety net among us. In the name of Christ Jesus. Amen.

Prayer for a Son or Daughter with an Addiction

SUGGESTED READING: PROVERBS 23:29–35

———◈———

Lord of freedom, thank You for being with us in the most dramatic moments of our lives. We never thought we'd see problems like these. We have a child who has fallen into an addiction and does not have the strength to get out. He (she) lies to himself (herself) and spiritual weakness does not allow him (her) to move forward. He (she) is destroying himself (herself) physically, emotionally, and spiritually.

Lord, help him (her). Free him (her) from this bondage. Please also guide our family because we are all affected. Soothe us and help us to recall that we can count on You. Motivate us by Your Word so that we make the right decisions regarding treatment. May the love that brings us together not be weakened by fear and mistrust, but rather strengthened and affirmed by Your presence. May the example of Christ, who gave His life for us despite our lowly state, inspire us to give all we can to overcome and cure the wounds of our child. Remain with us amid this darkness that has fallen over our house, so that Your light may illuminate our minds and strengthen our hearts. In the name of Christ Jesus, God of freedom. Amen.

MY FAMILY

My Church

Thank You for My Brothers and Sisters in the Faith

SUGGESTED READING: 1 JOHN 4:7–12

⚬⚬⚬

Heavenly Father, source of all love, thank You for the pleasant company of my brothers and sisters in the faith. I am grateful that we share a common conviction in Your Word and that we can worship You together. Thank You because even despite differences and disagreements, we have learned to persevere and to get along. I am grateful that we have learned to obey Your command to love each other as brothers and sisters.

Thank You for teaching us to love one another as Christ loved us. Thank You for this love that serves as a testimony to the world of our faith. I am grateful that this love is for my good and causes me to grow. Thank You that my love can also be a help to my brothers and sisters, edifying them and easing their burdens. Lord, thank You that I have these brothers and sisters in the faith so close to me; You have called them and they are here by Your will. Lord, thank You for the good times and the bad that we have shared. Bless our caring relationship, which is born of You. In Christ's name. Amen.

I Have Doubts about My Friend's Faith

SUGGESTED READING: ACTS 9:26–28

⸺◈⸻

Almighty Lord, through Your Holy Spirit You can change the life of any human being. I believe that, but my friend's change of behavior seems suspicious to me. He (she) says he (she) has come to believe in You and that his (her) life is changed, but I think he (she) is imitating something that he (she) neither believes or feels. I have many fears and doubts about this situation. In any case, I may be mistaken, Lord. That is why I am asking You to help me accept this. Let me give my friend the chance to be different and let me see Your transformation in him (her). I know that he (she) might take some steps in the wrong direction, but it really is not fair of me to be mistrustful because of my own fears. I realize that Your Holy Spirit is free to act in different ways in each individual and to produce unique reactions and fruits in each of us. Help me not to discriminate against believers simply because they do not do what I do or say what I am expect. Teach me to pray for them and with them to learn to see Your glory. Lord, motivate me to help my friend so that we may grow in the faith and confess our fears to each other, so that we might have an open and sincere relationship. In the name of Christ, the Savior of both of us. Amen.

I Am Going to Take Holy Communion

SUGGESTED READING: 1 CORINTHIANS 11:23–28

—◦◦◦—

Lord of the mysteries of faith, today I will participate in the Lord's Supper, which You have instituted in order to give me concrete proof of Your love. Many questions tend to come to mind when I attempt to explain what I am doing. Yet faith has allowed me to accept and obey Your commandment to do this in memory of Jesus.

May this Sacrament that I am going to receive help me to feel more certain that I am Your child, that You love me, and that You want to use me to share the Gospel. Thank You for allowing me to participate in this service with my brothers and sisters in the faith. May their presence and their need for You and their faith also build me up. Bless them so that we may feel united in You, just as Your disciples did. In Christ's name. Amen.

Prayer for the Evangelists
SUGGESTED READING: 2 TIMOTHY 4:1–5

———

Heavenly Father, who desires the salvation of all people, I want to ask You to be with all evangelists. May they use the gift that You have given them in a responsible way because it is a charge given by You. Teach them to be persistent in their work and to seek the best opportunities for sharing the Gospel. Help them to calmly tolerate difficult people who prefer to hear stories and myths rather than the truth of Your Word. May they not become depressed because of this, because it is one of the reactions that we can expect Your Word to receive.

Make them feel the presence of Your Holy Spirit so that they will not feel forgotten. May they have wisdom to speak and to remain silent, being prudent with their words so that they might not close the doors of anyone's heart.

Bless them, Lord, with the power that Your Holy Spirit gives, so that they might fulfill their ministry with enthusiasm and zeal and rejoice with those who are saved. In Christ's name, who has given us this command. Amen.

Prayer for My Pastor
SUGGESTED READING: HEBREWS 13:17

L ord of pastors, thank You for our pastor who builds us up with the message of Your Word. Thank You because he prays for Your care in our lives and heals us by bringing forgiveness to bind up the wounds of our souls. I appreciate that he directs the church that You established here so that our faith may be strengthened and that we might serve You with joy.

I pray that You encourage our pastor to continue in his work. May he be able to work with joy and without complaining, because complaints are useless. If he makes mistakes, help us not to notice them or to correct them humbly. If he has weaknesses, help us to make an effort to meet those needs. You have called us to work together. Sometimes it is hard for us to understand each other because we have different gifts. But we can grow in Your love and learn to respect each other with our strengths and weaknesses.

Lord, I beg You that Your Holy Spirit would uphold his trust and strength in Your Word so that he might guide us always in Your will. Teach us to submit to one another in love and to show gestures of appreciation and mutual acceptance. In the name of Christ, the Shepherd of shepherds. Amen.

Prayer for the Indifference of Some Members

SUGGESTED READING: LUKE 13:1–9

⎯⎯⎯✸⎯⎯⎯

Lord of patience, I pray for the members of our church. I especially pray for those members who do not want to participate in the activities of the church and who, despite invitations that we have given them, remain indifferent and disinterested. We begin to feel a desire to kick them out of our community, but we understand that we ought to be patient with them and to seek their return to Your house.

As a church, help us to not consider ourselves superior, because someday we may also become distanced. Help us to pray for them with love and concern. Help us to dig around and to fertilize that fig tree so that it may bear fruit. Guide us with wisdom so that we may find the best way to share Your Word. We beg that Your Holy Spirit would touch their hearts and allow them to recognize their lack of sincerity in living out their faith. Lord, we trust in Your power to cause children to return to their Father. In the name of Christ. Amen.

Prayer on the Day of Baptism
SUGGESTED READING: MATTHEW 3:13–17

———∽∽∽———

Heavenly Father, God of our salvation, today we come before Your presence in great joy and fear that through the means of Your Sacrament of Holy Baptism You might purify the soul of this person and receive him (her) as Your child. We are moved to do so by the great love You have shown us in Jesus. He died for our sins and rose to give us new life. He sent His disciples into all the world to baptize in Your name so that all might have this forgiveness and new life.

Although Baptism seems like a simple act in our eyes, the Holy Spirit gives the water and the Word a transcendent and eternal worth. Give us faith to firmly trust in Your promises and to be obedient to You. May this day of new birth bring lasting joy to our lives so that we may die daily to all evil, to be reborn into goodness. In the name of Christ, the author of salvation. Amen.

Prayer for the Preacher

SUGGESTED READING: LUKE 4:16–22

—∞—

L ord of inspiration, thank You because we have
someone to preach Your Word and to help us to
know Your will. You have given him the ability to
understand Your message and to communicate it in
the best way so that we can understand and reflect
on it.

I want to pray for the preacher of Your Word so that
You would bring him a sense of peace; may his mind be
clear and able to choose the right words to express the
message You have placed in his heart. Help him that
so his message might be pleasing and cause everyone's
ears to be opened to hear it. May he know how to reach
our hearts with the force of the Law as well as with the
sweet message of the Gospel. Encourage the Holy Spirit
to inspire him and encourage him to be convinced of the
importance of his message in order to share it enthusias-
tically with his audience. Let his mind focus on this task
instead of on any personal problems that may be worrying him. May his message encourage his faith and ours.
In the name of Christ Jesus. Amen.

Prayer for Missions

SUGGESTED READING: ROMANS 1:8–17

·——⊗⊗⊗——·

Heavenly Father, Savior of the nations, You want people from around the globe to have the chance to hear Your message of salvation. For this reason we pray for the church's missions that work to extend the reach of the Gospel. Guide the leaders who work in this field so that they do not become discouraged by rejection and indifference, and that with creativity and wisdom, they might find ways to channel their efforts to carry Your message. May the Holy Spirit accompany them in their daily work, and may they enjoy the wonderful experience of seeing Your transforming power in action in the lives of those who do not yet know the Gospel.

Remove every political, social, and economic obstacle that impedes missionaries from working freely. Protect them from evil and from the dangers of spiritual warfare. May Your Word and the experiences of the apostles encourage them to keep preaching with the conviction that a little bit of leaven can cause the whole loaf to rise. May they overcome their uncertainties and take advantage of opportunities. In the name of Christ, the Lord of our mission. Amen.

On Preparing a Christmas Program

SUGGESTED READING: LUKE 2:8–20

Lord of Christmas, I am grateful that Christmas is coming soon and that I can remember the wonderful news of Jesus' birth. Thank You for this time of joy and love. Let the words and actions of our church members reflect the sense of peace and forgiveness of this season.

Lord, help us to find the best way to communicate this wonderful message to the people who will join us this year to celebrate Christmas. May we sing hymns with joy that comes from the heart. May our messages, well-wishes, and Christmas program all be full of sincerity and love. May church members, as well as our pastors, be moved by the marvelous news of the birth of Jesus our Savior to give glory and praise to the God of our salvation.

Help us to spread this enthusiasm that Your Spirit has awakened within us to each one of the participants in our Christmas program. May each participant make a meaningful contribution, and may we leave behind old grudges and fatigue and be willing to meet the loving and peaceful Child of Bethlehem anew. In the name of Jesus, our Savior. Amen.

Prayer for the Pastor's Family
SUGGESTED READING: 1 TIMOTHY 5:17–25

Heavenly Father, who calls pastors to lead us to grow in faith, thank You for the pastor whom You have placed in our congregation, who day by day watches over our souls. I am grateful that he studies the Scripture and seeks the best ways to teach, exhort, and nourish us. I ask for Your forgiveness for the times that I have made his work more difficult with my complaints and reproaches because afterwards I noticed he became sad and discouraged.

I pray for his and his family's well-being. Protect them from every evil and danger because the devil seeks to destroy his work and reputation in many ways, even by attacking his family. Allow us to understand that even though he is an example to all in his lifestyle, he is also capable of making mistakes and sinning just like the rest of us. I pray for his wife and his children so that they may feel comfortable among us and that they may grow in the Gospel. May they feel motivated to support his ministry by understanding his schedule and his responsibilities. May they not consider the pastor's job to be a burden but rather a beautiful privilege. Encourage us to follow his example of a Christian life, for the salvation of others. In Christ's name, who gave everything for us. Amen.

Prayer for Seminary Students
SUGGESTED READING: JOHN 1:35–51

⸻

Lord of our vocations, thank You for those whom You have called to serve You full time and who have decided to study and prepare themselves by attending the seminary. Their gifts and expectations are different, as well as their experiences in the faith. But since You have a purpose for their lives, give them the conviction that is only obtained with the study of Your Word and the enabling presence of the Holy Spirit.

Protect them; prevent them from giving up or become discouraged because of the obstacles that they will encounter along their way. May they overcome their theological and personal doubts, so that these might be just steps in their journey of faith and not stumbling blocks that would hold them back. Give them the ability to adapt to different circumstances and to overcome the melancholy and longing of being homesick for their families. I especially pray that You would make their joy in serving You more intense and new than anything else in this world so that nothing would cause them to abandon You. In the name of Jesus, who has called them to this exciting adventure. Amen.

Prayer for Sunday School Teachers

SUGGESTED READING: MATTHEW 18:10–14

~~~

Lord of teaching and Father of the children, thank You for the teachers that You have called to work with the children in Sunday School. We are grateful that they share their time and talents in Your service for the love of the children. Thank You because they see how important it is that the children become familiar with Your Word as soon as possible so that they may enjoy life to the full.

I pray that You would give them creativity to prepare their classes; understanding to listen to the problems of these small voices; patience to guide and correct them according to the Lord's teachings; and love to share with the lonely of heart, the hurting, the detached, and the victims of abuse.

You are able to provide them with everything they need in order to meet the needs of these children. May Your Word nourish our teachers, may prayer come to their assistance, and may the Holy Spirit encourage and uplift them. May the other believers recognize their work and make it easier for them. May they enjoy the fruits of their labor as teachers. In the name of Jesus, the friend of little children. Amen.

Prayer for Seminary Professors
SUGGESTED READING: ACTS 5:34–40

⁂

Lord of Wisdom, thank You for the professors who teach theology. They have a great and important responsibility since they prepare the future leaders of the Church. Help them to seek new and better ways of teaching God's Word.

Bless each of them in their particular fields of study. They are all equally important in the development of their studies. Guide them as they give their classes so that they might offer the best of what they have to give. May they prepare their classes with enthusiasm and dedication, knowing that they do it for You. May they feel the Church's appreciation for their work. Help them to care about the personal integrity of their students and not just their academic preparation. Encourage them with Your Spirit to seek new and different ways to teach so that the Bible might keep its freshness and newness in our present day. Bless their efforts; bless their families; and help them in their personal struggles. Give them the ability and intelligence to understand their readings; give them the peace and rest of Your presence for their tired hands and minds. May they maintain enthusiasm for their work, knowing that what they sow will yield fruit. In Christ's name. Amen.

I Have a Friend Who Is Angry with the Pastor

SUGGESTED READING: 3 JOHN 9–11

Lord of reconciliation, thank You for Your forgiveness. We appreciate You for what You teach us and what You do to make us live in peace with You and with one another. Thank You that the mediation of Jesus Christ has made reconciliation with You possible, and because His mediation can aid reconciliation.

I pray for my friend who is angry with the pastor. They have different ways of seeing things and their own ways of responding. I do not know who is right. I respect and appreciate both of them, and I do not want to see them at odds with each other and fighting. Give me the right words to help them to think. Give me listening ears to hear their differences, and a peaceful spirit so that I do not judge their actions. Let me share with them the beautiful example of Jesus Christ, who gave up who He was in order to bring us peace. May Your Holy Spirit ignite the love and humility that Christ has placed in their hearts. In His name. Amen.

For Those Who Are Angry at the Church
SUGGESTED READING: EXODUS 17:1–7

～∞～

Heavenly Father, who hears our prayers and supplications and meets our every need, I pray for those who are at odds with the church. Their complaints about the work that we do have reached such a level that they do not see Your presence or Your company. In the weakness of their faith, they have not seen Your hand and Your support, and they have become angry with the pastor.

It is difficult, Lord, to talk with them without having lots of complaints and protests arise. Lord, help me to not become weary of praying that they might see that You have always cared about their needs and that, despite our unfaithfulness, You always remain faithful to Your promise of love and mercy. May these difficult circumstances that have arisen not divide us once again but rather give us proof that Your love remains intact. Lord, calm their extreme sensitivity; may they see things in a realistic way. Help our love for Christ and the obedience to Your Word be first in our lives to motivate us to get rid of these resentments. In the name of Christ, the Lord, who brings peace to our souls. Amen.

Prayer for the Missionaries
SUGGESTED READING: COLOSSIANS 4:2–4

Lord of the mission, thank You for missionaries whom You have called to be Your messengers in new places where the Gospel hasn't reached yet. Thank You for giving them the gifts they need in order to do their work, and thank You for nourishing their faith despite persecutions, rejection and mockery. Keep them from all kinds of evil so that they might work freely and communicate the message of salvation.

I pray especially for missionaries of our church. May the loneliness that they sometimes feel be eased by Your wonderful presence. May the anxiety to get a response to Your Gospel be calmed by the sure presence of the Holy Spirit. Give them the ability to take advantage of all the opportunities that come about, and help them to seek the best ways to communicate the message. May they harvest in joy what they have sometimes had to sow with tears. Strengthen them, Lord, so that they might serve You and thus bring others to know the salvation that You have given us in Christ Jesus. In the name of the Lord of the mission. Amen.

Prayer for Women

SUGGESTED READING: ACTS 9:36–43

〜∞〜

Lord of men and women, thank You for the women who have received Your salvation and who use their gifts in Your service. We are grateful that in addition to their family, work, and civil duties, they seek to grow constantly in the knowledge of Your Word and in their faith. Thank You that according to the gifts that You've given them as women, they can serve the church and their neighbor with creativity, joy and good will.

Lord, bless them with Your wisdom so that they might be able to discern Your will for the present moment. May they feel Your love and care in what they are doing so that they can do it willingly. Help them to grow in fellowship and in cooperation as they work on projects that require everyone's cooperation. Many women have served You with humility and dedication. May their examples inspire the women of our church to seek their own ways of serving You. In the name of Christ Jesus. Amen.

Prayer for Maundy Thursday
SUGGESTED READING: MARK 14:22–25

—⧼⧽—

Heavenly Father, Lord of mysteries, thank You for this Holy Thursday in which we remember the wonderful love of Christ made manifest for us. Thank You because in memory of Him and the Last Supper, we are able to receive Jesus' body and blood in the bread and wine. In this mystery of the faith You strengthen our love.

On this tragic Thursday that begins in celebration and ends in grief, may we be aware of our sins that Christ took upon Himself for our sake. May we remember that His silence and His submission were for our benefit and our liberation. Help us to seek holiness in our lives with solemnity and meditation. May we remember His betrayal, His abandonment, and the bitter solitude of that night, and may we meditate once again on our own failures as God's children. Help us to be aware of our vulnerability in the face of sin and the need we have for the Holy Spirit to remain firm in Him.

When we receive the bread and wine, the body and blood of Jesus, may we feel at one with Him in His death and resurrection. In His name. Amen.

Prayer for Vicars and for Their Pastoral Practice

SUGGESTED READING: MATTHEW 10:5–15

⟨⟨⟨⟩⟩⟩

Lord of servanthood, thank You for all those who study and prepare themselves to serve in Your Church. Thank You for the students who are getting ready to put what they have learned into practice. Be with them as they take their first steps, since they are likely to be full of fear and enthusiasm. Help them in the joys and struggles that they may find the right words for every situation.

Encourage them with Your Spirit in the moments of weakness and discouragement. Give them patience during conflict. Forgive the mistakes they make. May their perseverance and their faithfulness in serving You keep them motivated. Protect them from every kind of evil and danger that will be used by the devil to lead them away from their calling. May their daily devotions and their meditation on Your Word and prayer be the source of help to them during their time of practice. May they be humble and learn to submit to their superiors in order to learn from those who have gone before them along the same way. May they keep Christ's recommendations in mind for all those who are called to preach the coming of the Kingdom. In His name. Amen.

Prayer in Gratitude
for the Help of Another Church

SUGGESTED READING: 2 CORINTHIANS 8:1–7

———∞∞∞———

Lord of generosity and mutual help, thank You for granting us salvation. Your mercy and Your love know no limits. Your grace is abundant, varied, and diverse.

Thank You for moving us to help each other as brothers and sisters in the faith, bridging distances of time and space.

We thank You for the brothers and sisters in the faith who, with their prayers and offerings, have helped us so that we could come to faith in You and grow in that faith. We are grateful for their sacrifice and love for Your sake. Bless their willingness and their love for us.

You have promised to give us Your grace in abundance so that we also have plenty to share with others. We have seen this grace in our brothers and sisters and we are very grateful for their witness. Help us to follow their example and to be grateful and responsible in using their gifts. In the name of Christ, our generous Teacher. Amen.

Prayer for Other Christian Churches
SUGGESTED READING: ROMANS 15:20-21

———∞∞———

Lord of the Church, I believe in one holy Christian Church that transcends the limits of doctrines, that You know those who belong to You, and that You hope that Your Word will extend to the very ends of the earth.

Thank You for believers in other Christian churches who also seek to spread the message of salvation. Teach us to respect one another and to hold the work You carry out among all of us in high regard. Do not allow religious fanaticism and intolerance to lead us to close ourselves off or to criticize others harshly in ways that reflect badly on the Lord in whom we trust.

Time and circumstances have made us how we are. But beyond our different ways of serving You, we know we are united by the same Holy Spirit. Lord, teach us to be tolerant among us, to cultivate understanding and mutual respect, and above all, to be faithful to Your Word. In the name of Christ, Master of unity. Amen.

We Have a New Pastor

SUGGESTED READING: 1 TIMOTHY 3:1–7

———— ❦ ————

Lord of the Church, thank You for giving us a new pastor for our congregation. It is been difficult to work without having a spiritual leader. Thank You for calling the right person, despite our fears, doubts, demands, and appearances.

Help him to adjust to this new place. May we remember that we should be cooperative and respectful of his position. Cultivate friendship among us and make us faithful listeners to his teaching. Teach us to be forgiving and to accept his limitations and mistakes so that we might be able to work well together for Your kingdom.

Your work is great: it is important and it requires moral fortitude from those in leadership. May Your Holy Spirit help our pastor's faith grow as he serves as our guide to strengthening our own. May he be a faithful witness for those who do not yet know the Gospel. In the name of Christ, the Pastor of pastors. Amen.

Prayer for the Pastor's Wife
SUGGESTED READING: 1 CORINTHIANS 9:1–14

———

Lord of those whom You send forth, we thank You for the pastor whom You have called for our congregation, and we are thankful for his family. Thank You for the support and companionship that his wife provides. Bless her that she may feel content and at home in this congregation so that we might be helpful in her growing in faith.

Assist her when she has to wait for her husband to come home because he is needed for work. Give her wisdom when she has to make urgent decisions about tasks that he has left undone. May she pray with patience and not live in a big hurry so that he can find rest and peace at home. May her example inspire other women in the congregation to serve God with joy.

Strengthen her faith so that she can accept the pastoral ministry as an exciting adventure in the faith that does not just bring demands but that also brings beautiful privileges. May she be a good companion at home and an attentive partner in the pastoral work. In Christ's name. Amen.

Prayer for a Bible Study

SUGGESTED READING: PSALMS 19:7–14

———∞∞∞———

Lord of new life in Christ, thank You for giving Your Word as a source of meditation so that we might obtain the wisdom, joy and encouragement that we need to live a new life.

Awaken within believers the interest to grow in the knowledge of Your Word so that they will be on guard from deception and know how to live according to Your will. May they overcome their fears and may the Spirit open their eyes and their understanding so that our faith might grow through the study of Your Word. Faith comes through hearing, and hearing from the Word of God. Help us to get to know You better, the God of love and salvation, and to also know ourselves better, since we often live in denial with our own preconceived notions.

Lord, help us to diligently cultivate our minds and hearts with an intensive study of Your Word, which is alive and effective, and help us to change what we cannot change in ourselves. In the name of Christ Jesus, Lord of wisdom and source of joy and confidence. Amen.

There Are Problems in the Church
SUGGESTED READING: 1 CORINTHIANS 1:10–17

L ord of unity, thank You for my congregation. Here is where I came to faith in Christ, and here is where I learned to serve You. But recently some rivalries and divisions among the members have appeared. People try to impose their own opinion rather than seeking reconciliation with others, and they have abandoned the humility of recognizing their own faults.

The majority of the members do not want to participate in the activities anymore. They just talk about the problems that exist. The pastor has tried to reconcile the brothers and sisters, but people take things the wrong way, creating misunderstandings. Lord, I ask for Your wisdom and for a great measure of brotherly love to bring a resolution to this situation. It is evident that evil has come among us. Give us strength to keep working to seek peace and unity. May we remember that we were all saved by the same Lord and called to be part of this body by the same Spirit. Help us to not encourage or feed the divisions that are mounting.

Help us recognize our mistakes and to be humble. May Your example of love and respect motivate us to be put up with each other and to reconcile our differences. In Christ's name, the head of our church. Amen.

My Pastor Doesn't Preach Well

SUGGESTED READING: 2 TIMOTHY 2:14–21

———∞∞∞———

Lord of gifts and talents, thank You for the pastor whom You have placed in our congregation. We are grateful that he directs and guides the work of the whole church so that we remain true to the faith and so that we can reach others with the message of salvation. Thank You for his witness and his abilities. However, I want to pray that You help us to find a way to help him with his preaching. It is evident that it is hard for him, and he suffers a lot when he has to preach in front of the congregation. He cannot find the right words to express himself well, and he lacks the skills needed for researching the Bible as well.

I know that not everyone has the same gifts to meet all the needs that our institutions sometimes demand. But in the Scriptures You show us many people who served You in spite of their limitations. Help us as a congregation to speak with him and to help him in the event that he needs special training. May we be able to talk with him about this, and may we also grow in the ministry of God's kingdom. May Your Holy Spirit, who provides the church with the gifts that it needs, guide us to make the right decisions for everyone. In Christ's name. Amen.

It is the Month of the Bible
SUGGESTED READING: 2 TIMOTHY 3:14–17

—❧—

L ord of the Word, I thank You because in all times You have raised up people who have given written testimony about Your action toward Your people, who You have saved through Your great love. We appreciate that these writings have been collected because they are useful to us today, through the work of the Holy Spirit, as a guide for living according to Your will. We are grateful to be able to rely on the Bible.

Bless those who work in the translation of the Scriptures to bring Your Word to all people in their own language. Thank You for those who seek to adapt the language of the Bible to children and youth so that they can also know Your message of salvation. Bless the ministries of Bible societies, of editors, and of bookstores that facilitate sharing the Bible. Obstruct the plans of those who seek to impede the distribution of Your Word. Motivate each believer to value this treasure, using it daily to grow in the knowledge of Your will to teach, to correct, and to learn to do good. Thank You, Lord, because we know You thanks to the Bible's witness. In Christ's name. Amen.

A Pastoral Conference

SUGGESTED READING: 1 PETER 5:1–4

Heavenly Father, Lord of pastors, thank You for this opportunity that pastors have to gather at this conference. Thank You because You have cared for them in their ministry, blessed their work, prepared them, and have offered Your aid to overcome the temptations and dangers they have encountered in their work.

Bless this conference so that they may have the space and time to share their experiences, heal their hurts, strengthen their ties of friendship and faith, and find answers and encouragement for the challenges they face in their family and in their personal lives. In Your Word and through prayer, may they find the rest and encouragement they need to enjoy their work. Help them to correct their mistakes and learn from one another so they may carry out their work with enthusiasm and good will. Bless their families, care for them and protect them. May Your Holy Spirit fill these pastors with humility to give and receive advice from one another. In the name of Christ, who often went away to rest with His disciples and to encourage one another in their work. Amen.

Prayer for the Choir

SUGGESTED READING: PSALM 149:1–6

※

L ord of praise, thank You for the choir in which I am able to participate. Thank You for our director who leads us in song. Give him (her) the ability he (she) needs to teach and guide us in the hymns and songs that we sing. Thank You for this gift that You have given us that we enjoy and put to service for You.

Bless the work of the choir so that we may practice new songs that praise Your name. May we give faithful witness to our gratitude for the salvation and new life that You have given us through Christ Jesus. Help us to overcome our fears and limitations, to sing with joy and tranquility, to breathe and to raise our voices. Give us the ability to express different feelings through music and singing and to cultivate faith and call for reflection. May we praise You and give You glory with the enthusiasm that belongs to a grateful people. Help us to accept correction. Help us to listen to each other since that is how we make harmony, the most beautiful sound to Your ears. May our voices proclaim Your wonders. In the name of Christ, our great wonder. Amen.

Prayer for the Church Council
SUGGESTED READING: EXODUS 18:13-27

——∞——

Lord of order and peace, thank You for those believers who give their time and talents to serve others in the church council. Give them Your blessing so that they may serve with joy and enthusiasm, knowing that they are doing it for You and for the expansion of Your kingdom. Give them wisdom to make the right decisions as they face challenges. Protect them from indifference and from the fears that tend to overcome those who provide leadership to an institution.

Allow them to gain experience, to investigate and to strengthen their faith so that they may direct the church as You have called them to as leaders. May Your Word encourage and challenge them when they feel unmotivated, may Your Holy Spirit console them when they feel criticized and misunderstood, and may prayer keep them humble in their relationship with You and with the church.

Father, You have called leaders who coordinate the work in an orderly and peaceful way for Your church; accompany each of those whom You have called so that they may enjoy this time of serving on the church council. In the name of Christ, the head of our church. Amen.

Today I Will Share Christ with Someone
SUGGESTED READING: ACTS 16:25–33

Lord of salvation, thank You for the privilege You have given me of sharing the Gospel with someone who does not know it. I know that this is also a great responsibility, and I do not want to waste it. Lord, give me a peaceful and humble mind to listen carefully and to respond with love and respect. May I use Your Word and respond well to questions in order to open the way for the work of the Holy Spirit.

I am very anxious. Help me to remember that the Spirit will give me the words that I need in the moment, and that it is Your presence alone that can cause repentance of sins and faith in Christ as Savior. Lord, help me to leave the door open for a new opportunity in case what we desire does not happen this time. This beautiful privilege that You have given me can be something that could change the life of this person forever. Help me to do my part responsibly and to trust that You will do Your work through the Holy Spirit. I beg this in the name of Christ my Savior. Amen.

Election of the Church Council
SUGGESTED READING: ACTS 6:1–7

Heavenly Father, You choose and call those You need to lead Your Church. We pray that You would preside over this assembly that gathers in my church that each one of us might, with a clean conscience, in good will, and with reverence and fear, be attentive to Your call to serve in Your kingdom.

Help us to recognize the great love that You have shown us in saving us and making us part of Your Church. Awaken within us the desire to serve You with the gifts that You have given us, so that we can help each other to grow. Take away selfishness and indifference that can lead us to seek only our own benefit without noticing the needs of others.

May there be a spirit of dedication, gratitude, and willingness to offer our best to You. Guide us, Lord, to choose the brothers and sisters whom You have prepared for Your service. May we be respectful of the majority's opinion, recognizing that Your Holy Spirit is acting through us for the well-being of all. May each one, according to his conscience and through prayer, consider what is best for the whole Church. Through Jesus Christ, the Lord of our church. Amen.

For the Call of a Pastor
SUGGESTED READING: ACTS 1:23–26

‒‒‒∽∾‒‒‒

Heavenly Father, who through the Church calls those You have chosen for Your service, You have established various ministries to develop the work of the Church. You have raised up apostles, evangelists, prophets, pastors and teachers to whom You have given the gifts needed to serve Your Church. Guide us in the selection and calling of a pastor for our congregation. Give us good judgment so that we may see the work we do as well as the needs we have in a realistic and sincere way. Help us to think with clarity about the gifts of those whom we have proposed to meet. You have already prepared a pastor to work in this place. We must now follow Your advice and Your will to call the right one.

When the call is made, cause the pastor to meditate on it under the guidance of Your Holy Spirit with the same gravity and respect that we are doing. In this way, all our work may be according to Your holy will. We ask this in the name of Jesus Christ. Amen.

Prayer for the Unity of the Church
SUGGESTED READING: EPHESIANS 2:17–22

⸻⸻

L ord of the Church, thank You for calling me to be part of Your church, in this family of brothers and sisters. Thank You that You unite us through one Spirit and that we enjoy the very peace that Jesus has given us.

You have called us into this church from different places and over many years. Some were closer and some were further away when You called us through Your Holy Spirit. But now you have knit us together as a family, one church in which we learn to love each other. Forgive us for our discord and disharmony. Motivate us to seek unity and peace in Christ above all, which are the ties that we need most. You know the reason and the purpose for which You have founded this church in this place. Reveal Your purpose to us so that we may act in accordance with Your will.

Father God, Father of this family, cause the bonds attained by our Brother Jesus to be strengthened through Your Holy Spirit that we may serve You in the best way. In Christ's name. Amen.

Before Deciding My Offering
SUGGESTED READING: 2 CORINTHIANS 9:7–11

Heavenly Father, Lord of gifts, thank You for all the blessings I have received. Thank You that my family has not lacked food or clothing. Thank You for my health and work and that my relationship with my family has been loving and forgiving. Thank You for Your patience with me when I stray and make mistakes. Thank You for Your protection.

However, there have been times when I have wished for a more blessed and abundant life. But I trust that despite the shortages that we have had, Your wise and protective hand has been there.

Lord, give me a grateful and contented spirit so that I might thankfully and gratefully decide how much to give. May my offering be one of good will, without fear, and with great faith, knowing that You will not allow me to be lacking in anything I need.

Your Son Jesus gave all He had for our salvation. May my offering be motivated by the grace that I have received in You and by the desire that others may also receive Christ's salvation. Teach me to be generous and to trust in You. In His name I ask this. Amen.

We Are Having an Election
SUGGESTED READING: ACTS 6:105

———∞∞∞———

Lord of calls and elections, be present with us on this election day, that we may carefully consider the abilities of each person who might occupy a post and carry out the tasks of service that each job requires. Motivate us to pray and to respect those who are elected by the majority.

May their ideas and efforts prosper, that they might develop their gifts. May we keep in mind the spirit of servanthood that characterizes the children of God and not try to flee from the responsibilities that might be asked of us according to the gifts that You have given. May we be willing to accept the responses of those who cannot accept a nomination because of just reasons. Inspire us by Your Holy Spirit to seek everyone's well-being in this selection process. We ask this in the name of Jesus Christ, who taught us to pray before He chose His disciples. Amen.

Index of Prayers